Wired to Move

A STARTING POINT PUBLICATION

By Ruth Hanford Morhard

Foreword by Larry Griffin

Introductions by Anthony President and
Felix Muniz, DMin

A *STARTING POINT PUBLICATION*

Starting Point is a Cleveland, Ohio-based nonprofit child care, early education, and youth services agency with a long history of innovative initiatives, many of them models for early childhood programs in Ohio and across the nation.

In 2010, Starting Point began a landmark Boys' Project to address the unique issues surrounding boys three to six years old, prompted by data on the disproportionate numbers of boys with social/emotional behavior and learning challenges and concerns, particularly in the African American and Hispanic/Latino communities. This book was created to help teachers better understand, support, and work with these young boys.

The Starting Point Boys' Project is under the direction of

- Billie Osborne-Fears, Starting Point Executive Director

- Constance Walker, Starting Point Special Needs Child Care Coordinator and Boys' Project Manager.

GH10035
A Gryphon House Book

Wired

TO MOVE

Facts and
Strategies for
Nurturing
Boys in an
Early
Childhood
Setting

Ruth Hanford Morhard

**for Starting Point for Child Care
and Early Education**

A

PUBLICATION

Foreword by Larry Griffin

Introductions by Anthony President and Felix Muniz, DMin

**Gryphon House, Inc.
Lewisville, NC**

Library of Congress Cataloging-in-Publication Data

Morhard, Ruth Hanford.
 Wired to move : facts and strategies for nurturing boys in an early childhood
setting / by Ruth Hanford Morhard ; foreword by Larry Griffin ; inroductions by
Anthony Presiden and Felix Muniz, DMin.
     pages cm
 ISBN 978-0-87659-322-6
1. Boys--Education (Early childhood) 2. Sex differences in education. I. Title.
 LC1390.M67 2013
 372.21--dc23
                                2013007692

Bulk Purchase

Gryphon House books are available for special premiums and sales promotions
as well as for fund-raising use. Special editions or book excerpts also can be
created to specifications. For details, contact the Director of Marketing at
Gryphon House.

Disclaimer

Gryphon House, Inc., cannot be held responsible for damage, mishap, or injury
incurred during the use of or because of activities in this book. Appropriate and
reasonable caution and adult supervision of children involved in activities and
corresponding to the age and capability of each child involved are recommended
at all times. Do not leave children unattended at any time. Observe safety and
caution at all times.

Table of Contents

DEDICATION

This book is dedicated to
- all the early childhood professionals who care for and support boys;
- all the parents who are trying to raise positive, healthy, productive, responsible boys; and
- all the wonderful young boys who will grow up to be wonderful men.

ACKNOWLEDGMENTS

We would like to thank the many people who not only have recognized that too many boys, especially African American and Hispanic/Latino boys, are falling behind in learning, but also are working to reverse the trend.

Starting Point staff, affiliated agencies, pilot programs, committees, and consultants put their hearts and souls into the Boys' Project as they do in everything they attempt—under the strong guidance of Constance Walker; the professional support of Michelle Bledsoe, Tameisha Redd, Iam, Andria Artist, Subhit Kodapully, and Julia Garber from Starting Point; Holli Ritzenthaler and Tamika Schaffer from Guidestone (formerly Berea Children's Home & Family Services); and Rebecca Volle, Kathleen Ruic, Naomi Smart, Michelle Lazroff, Sharon Gaspar, Fabiola Hysenaj, and the wonderful children and parents who participated in the Boys' Project pilot programs at the Guidestone Family Life Child Care Centers in Lakewood and Maple Heights, Ohio. Our appreciation extends to Case Western Reserve University for its invaluable assistance in data collection.

Early inspiration came from educational consultant Larry Griffin, who worked with us to educate early childhood professionals in boys' brain differences, and from contributors Anthony President and Felix Muniz, DMin, who helped us understand why African American and Hispanic/Latino boys need extra support and attention.

We are indebted to the educators, psychiatrists, and writers whose research and writings have further opened our minds to the issues surrounding boys' development, including Dr. Daniel Amen, Dr. Janice Hale-Benson, Dr. Louann Brizendine, Kathy Evans, Mary Ann Fuller, Michel Gurian, Abigail Norfleet James, Tony Griego Jones, Dr. Jawanza Kunjufu, Dr. Terry Neu, Eli Newberger, William S. Pollack, Barrie Thorne, Rich Weinfeld, and Richard Whitmire. Much of the information in this manual had its origins in their work.

We would also like to thank technical consultant Jim Flynn from the Positive Education Program Early Childhood Plus and the Starting Point Men in Early Childhood Committee for their valuable input, Claire Rundelli for organizing the Resources section, and to the many librarians and early childhood teachers who recommended good books for boys. Thanks also to Raymond Rundelli, Esq., of Calfee, Halter & Griswold for his valuable assistance in intellectual property issues, and to Larry Griffin, whose support and contributions to Starting Point and this book have been invaluable.

This book would not have been possible without the unflinching support of Kaplan Early Learning Company—in particular Clarissa Willis, who recognized early on the importance of a book on young boys, and Laura Laxton, the superb editor whose wise guidance has helped shape this book and enhance its worth to teachers. Special mention must go to Marieca Anthony, our Kaplan Early Learning Company representative, who has gone above and beyond her job responsibilities to champion the Boys' Project.

TO THE MANY WONDERFUL EARLY CHILDHOOD TEACHERS

You may wonder why we have written a book targeting boys ages three to six. The answers are clear. Too many boys are falling behind in school, partly due to gender, race, and ethnicity issues that we believe can and should be addressed in early childhood classrooms.

We realized the extent of the problem when we looked at data from our own early childhood programs in Greater Cleveland. In 2009, an alarming 72 percent of all Cuyahoga County, Ohio, children ages three to six who were identified with social/emotional problems were boys. Out of these boys, a full 59 percent were African American, up from 40 percent in the preceding 10-year period.

When we checked national statistics, we found this was not simply a local problem:

- On average, boys lag one to one-and-a-half years behind girls in reading and writing skills.[1]
- Boys are four-and-a-half times more likely to be expelled from preschool than girls; African American boys are twice as likely to be expelled as white European American and Hispanic/Latino boys.[2]
- In 2009, African American and white males ages 16–24 had significantly higher dropout rates (10.6 percent) than females (8.1 percent); Hispanic/Latino males the same ages had the highest overall dropout rates (19 percent) of any ethnic group.[3]

To help reverse this troubling trend in our own region, we initiated the Starting Point Boys' Project. We looked for answers to our many questions. Why were there such startling differences in boys' and girls' development in the early years? Why were the problems so much more acute among African American and Hispanic/Latino boys?

We consulted with experts on brain development, gender, race, and ethnicity differences. We met with male-serving and early education organizations. We pulled together the latest literature and research findings. What we discovered was that our early

---

1   Gurian, Michael, and Kathy Stevens. 2005. *The Minds of Boys: Saving Our Sons from Falling Behind in School and in Life.* San Francisco: Jossey-Bass.
2   Gilliam, Walter S. 2005. *Prekindergarteners Left Behind: Expulsion Rates in State Prekindergarten Systems.* New Haven, CT: Yale University Child Study Center.
3   Chapman, C., J. Laird, N. Ifill, and A. KewalRamani. 2011. *Trends in High School Dropout and Completion Rates in the United States: 1972–2009* (NCES 2012–006). U.S. Department of Education. Washington, DC: National Center for Education Statistics, accessed July 24, 2012. http://nces.ed.gov/pubs2012/2012006.pdf.

childhood classrooms simply were not designed for the ways boys learn or for the unique needs of at-risk African American and Hispanic/Latino boys. We needed to take a fresh look at our curricula, our classrooms, and our teaching strategies.

We pulled together a team to develop strategies to address the many issues surrounding boys in early education settings. Then, we tested these strategies in pilot programs in select early education settings in Cleveland. We developed a teachers' manual; trained technical assistants to work with center directors, teachers, and staff; and held professional development seminars on working with boys.

Finally, we measured the results, using the Devereux Early Childhood Assessment (DECA). In one year, the percentage of boys identified with concerns regarding self-control was cut in half. Boys identified with strengths rose in initiative from 6 to 41 percent, in self-control from 12 to 41 percent, and in attachment from 12 to 47 percent. Interestingly, girls' performance improved, too.

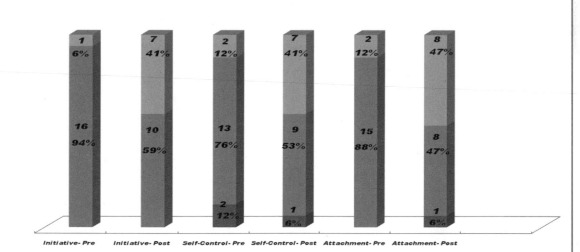

In this book, we share what we have learned, focusing on boys' brain differences and on the special issues affecting African American and Hispanic/Latino boys. You will find strategies and resources aimed at helping teachers transform early childhood classrooms from boy averse to boy friendly.

By implementing teaching strategies known to be effective and culturally informed, teachers will have better success in managing boys' challenging behaviors, addressing learning difficulties, and meeting the unique needs of African American and Hispanic/Latino boys. Our ultimate aims are to raise awareness and understanding of how boys learn and behave so that, together, we can start these boys on the path to new success in school and in life.

It is our hope that this book will be insightful, instructive, and inspirational.

Good luck!

Billie Osborne-Fears

Billie Osborne-Fears, Executive Director
Starting Point for Child Care and Early Education

FOREWORD
By Larry J. Griffin

As teachers, we have made huge strides in early childhood education. We understand the importance of the early years to a child's brain development. We know how critical our role is in preparing children to be successful in school. We eagerly seek out new information that will help us do our jobs better. Despite our best efforts, there is a hidden problem. Too many boys are falling behind. But why? I wanted to find out.

I thought back to my own early school experiences. I found it frustrating to keep still all day. More often than not, I complied—reluctantly—with the teacher's order to "stay in my seat." Other male classmates struggled even more. I vividly recall seeing boys singled out by teachers because they did not obey the rules. Most were simply energetic, inquisitive explorers. They found the classroom too confining. Slowly, they lost their enthusiasm for learning.

As a teacher, I have found that dealing with a boy's constant fidgeting, pushing, and running around can be quite challenging. If only we could bottle this "boy energy"—or contain it somehow! But, maybe containing it is not the answer. Perhaps containing it is part of the problem.

Studies show us boys are behind girls at every age level. Strikingly, this holds particularly true for preschool boys. In 2005, I became aware of a penetrating study on expulsion rates of preschool children, the National Prekindergarten Study (NPS), conducted by Walter Gilliam from Yale University. This study found that prekindergarten children in 2005-2006 public school-sponsored programs were expelled at a rate more than three times that of their older peers in K-12. Boys were at significantly higher risk—they were four-and-a-half times more likely to be expelled than girls. The statistics on minority boys were even worse—an alarming 90 percent of the African Americans expelled were boys.

The study validated a concern I have long held—that too many boys are not doing well in our current early learning environments. In their 2005 book, *The Minds of Boys: Saving Our Sons from Falling Behind in School and Life,* Michael Gurian and Kathy Stevens tell us that the average boy enters kindergarten up to a year and a half behind girls in language skills. That makes it hard for boys to keep pace with girls in learning environments where teachers use reading, writing, speaking, and listening skills to convey most of the information.

This is significant because boys account for 70 percent of all children diagnosed with learning disabilities. Even more disturbing, boys are four-and-a-half times more likely to be diagnosed with attention-deficit/hyperactivity disorder than girls. Eighty percent of all students taking Ritalin are boys. Gurian and Stevens observe that boys also represent 80 percent of students cited as discipline problems or diagnosed with behavioral disorders—a thought-provoking statistic.

If we look at whether boys' performance continues to lag behind girls' in our schools, National Center for Education statistics[4] for 2009 show us that a higher percentage of girls graduated from high school than boys. In addition, more than 10 percent of African American males and 19 percent of Hispanic/Latino males dropped out of school. Fewer boys than girls are now enrolled in college. The 2008 statistics indicate that less than half—43 percent—of students in the nation's college population are male. During the

---

4   Chapman et al. *Trends in High School Dropout and Completion Rates in the United States: 1972-2009.*

2008–2009 school year, women earned 57 percent of bachelor's degrees and 60 percent of master's degrees.

These statistics are troubling—for the future of our boys and our nation. But, at the same time, I believe we can halt these trends. Perhaps the problem has been more ours than theirs. We are learning more about how boys' brains function—that they are wired for some of the very things we teachers find frustrating. We are realizing that many of our early childhood classrooms are more suited to the way girls learn, and we are discovering that we can adapt the ways we work with boys to better fit their distinct learning styles.

> *Thousands of bright, energetic boys are spending the better part of each day unhappy and coming home to report to their parents that they feel "stupid" or that they "don't fit in."*
>
> *—BETH HERING,*
> **Helping Boys Get More Out of Elementary Education**

Some early care and education programs are addressing gender differences by modifying learning environments and activities to be more responsive to both male and female learning styles and preferences. Some are creating gender-specific, single-sex classrooms—one for boys and one for girls. They are finding that these approaches benefit both girls and boys.

Starting Point has taken a leading role in this endeavor with its comprehensive Boys' Project—training teachers on boys' brain differences, developing workable classroom strategies and materials, and evaluating the results. They are also addressing the acute learning needs of African American and Hispanic/Latino boys. In this book, Starting Point shares its knowledge, experience, and strategies in the hope that they will be valuable to early childhood teachers.

BOYS AND LEARNING[5, 6]

- *Prekindergarten boys are four-and-a-half times more likely to be expelled than girls.*

- *Of the African American children expelled, 90 percent are boys.*

- *In schools, 80 percent of discipline problems and 80 percent of children on Ritalin are boys.*

- *Boys are six months to one-and-a-half years behind girls in reading and writing at all elementary school levels.*

- *Boys get up to 70 percent of the Ds and Fs in most schools.*

- *Nearly twice as many boys as girls repeat a grade.*

- *In 2005, girls' grades overall averaged a B; boys', a C. Girls earned higher grade-point averages (GPAs) than boys (3.1 vs. 2.9).*

- *In 2007, boys' writing scores at all elementary school levels averaged 20 points lower than girls'.*

- *Males now represent only 43 percent of college students nationwide.*

---

5   Gurian and Stevens, *The Minds of Boys*, 22.

6   U.S. Department of Education, National Center for Education Statistics. 1992–2011. *National Assessment of Educational Progress* (NAEP), accessed November 1, 2011, from the Main NAEP Data Explorer. http://nces.ed.gov/nationsreportcard/naepdata

Larry J. Griffin is a dynamic speaker/presenter who draws from his experience in early education to make his presentations, keynotes, and trainings entertaining and relevant. He has done extensive research on brain-based gender differences and their practical implications for teachers of children from birth to five years old, and he presents this information to teachers, administrators, parents, and other professionals across the country. Griffin has a BA in early childhood and elementary education and an MEd in education administration with an emphasis in curriculum and instruction from the University of North Carolina at Charlotte (UNCC).

THE STARTING POINT BOYS' PROJECT

We created the Starting Point Boys' Project to address the growing disparity in boys' and girls' learning in the preschool years. We began by gathering information on the male brain; then, we took a fresh look at our programs—at our physical settings and at how we care for and teach young boys. Because the problems are more acute in African American and Hispanic/Latino boys, we paid special attention to the environments, cultures, and influences affecting them and developed additional strategies to address their unique needs.

As we developed our program, one thing became clear. Our current early childhood system, taught by mostly female teachers, tends to favor the abilities of girls, whose language and listening skills are better developed in the early years. The good news is that we are finding that simple changes can restore a balance. We know boys are not all the same. Many do well in typical early learning settings. What we have found is that there are significant differences in the way boys are wired that need to be taken into consideration when we are determining teaching methods and classroom arrangements. We also believe that we need to accommodate boys' needs in a way that enriches all the children in the classroom—girls as well as boys—building on their strengths, celebrating their cultures, and fostering the learning that will set successful patterns for their lives.

In the following pages, we share our findings and experience in adapting our programs to better meet the needs of boys. We offer insights and classroom strategies gleaned from the recommendations of leading experts in boys' learning; the results from our pilot Boys' Project sites; and input from early childhood experts from Starting Point, its affiliated agencies, consultants, and the Starting Point Men in Early Childhood Committee. We also include handouts and resources that we have found helpful in our quest to enhance boys' performance.

Through our Boys' Project, we have learned a great deal about boys in early childhood and how teachers can help them thrive in these all-important years. We hope this book will be useful to the countless dedicated early childhood teachers.

BOYS' PROJECT GUIDING PRINCIPLES

We believe that

- we must do our utmost to give boys the good start they need to be successful in school and beyond;
- we must continually seek ideas to improve the ways we teach and care for young boys, with special emphasis on disadvantaged or at-risk African American and Hispanic/Latino boys; and
- when we single out boys for special attention, we must make sure we do our best to nurture girls as well.

Following are the overall principles that guide our work with boys:

1. **Learn More about Boys**
   - Learn strategies for promoting boys' learning and development.
   - Exchange personal experiences with other teachers in the group to develop group rapport.
   - Be aware of how boys are doing in education and how they compare to female peers on academic indicators.
   - Understand the relationship between problems in early years and later outcomes.
   - Understand different views on the nature of learning and ability and the relationship to teachers' and students' behavior.
2. **Build Relationships**
   - Learn and use strategies for communicating and building relationships with boys from different racial and ethnic backgrounds.
   - Understand the importance of positive relationships with boys.

- Examine your own beliefs, values, and perceptions about boys of different backgrounds and how they might influence interactions with these boys.
- Understand boys' unique cultural and ethnic backgrounds, learning styles, behavior, and language and how they might interfere with relationship building.
- Learn new ways to interpret and respond to challenging boys' behaviors.

3. **Partner with Families**
   - Get to know the values, beliefs, norms, expectations, and practices of families.
   - Learn about and use appropriate approaches/strategies for reaching out to and communicating with families from diverse backgrounds.
   - Convey expectations to families and ask family members to share their expectations of the school and teacher.
   - Provide families with materials and strategies to support boys' learning at home.
   - Learn about and use strategies for having productive discussions with families about difficult subjects.
   - Strategize on how to foster/repair relationships and partner with "difficult" family members.
   - Create varied and multiple opportunities for family members to be involved in classroom activities, and encourage their participation.

4. **Make Classrooms More Boy Friendly**
   - Adapt classrooms to reflect boys' needs for movement and physical space.
   - Learn about and use strategies to address boys' brain differences and at-risk populations.
   - Incorporate superhero play.
   - Provide male role models as teachers, aides, speakers, and volunteers.
   - Encourage participation of fathers and father figures.

5. **Promote Social/Emotional Development**
   - Learn about and use appropriate boy-friendly strategies for social/emotional development.
   - Be sensitive and responsive to the emotional needs of boys.
   - Develop close, nurturing relationships with boys.

- Help boys learn to manage their aggressive and angry feelings appropriately.

6. **Address Challenging Behavior in the Classroom**
   - Identify different types and sources of challenging behavior in the classroom.
   - Structure the classroom environment to prevent or reduce challenging behaviors.
   - Learn and use strategies to reduce or redirect violence, aggression, and other types of challenging behavior "in the moment."
   - Learn ways to work with families to address difficult behavior.
   - Tap into school resources and other teachers as a source of support, information, and practical strategies.

7. **Promote Positive Racial, Ethnic, and Gender Identity**
   - Create opportunities for children to learn about and share information about their racial/ethnic heritage and culture.
   - Examine your own beliefs and values about racial, ethnic, and gender differences.
   - Create opportunities for students to learn about the work, family, and community experiences of positive male role models from minority backgrounds.
   - Be aware of how African American and Hispanic/Latino boys in your area are doing academically and how they compare to female and white peers on academic indicators. (See National Center for Education Statistics [nces.ed.gov fastfacts] and National Black Child Development Institute [http://nbcdi.org/] websites.)
   - Understand the unique backgrounds, learning styles, behavior, and language of African American and Hispanic/Latino boys that might interfere with relationship building and learning.
   - Learn and use strategies for communicating and building relationships with African American and Hispanic/Latino boys.
   - Be familiar with differences and similarities across contexts of development in discipline strategies, communication styles, language/dialect, and goals/expectations for African American and Hispanic/Latino boys.
   - Help African American and Hispanic/Latino boys develop positive racial and cultural identities when communicating with, motivating, and working with them.

WHAT LITTLE BOYS ARE MADE OF

Nature's Role

Just like the old nursery rhyme says, boys and girls are different. We have always known that. It is not just the obvious physical characteristics. Boys and girls are interested in different things. They think differently. They behave differently. Until recently, though, we did not have concrete evidence to tell us whether these differences were inborn or came from the way we raised our children. Were we teaching them to be different? Or did their DNA predispose them to take on certain roles?

The answer, of course, is both; however, we now are learning the precise role the brain plays in determining the characteristics of boys and girls.

*Frogs and snails and
puppy dog tails,
That's what little boys
are made of.
Sugar and spice and
everything nice,
That's what little girls
are made of.
—Mother Goose*

Some of these characteristics have evolved through thousands of years. In ancient times, before farming became the norm, men went out for long periods of time to hunt, fish, and defend their turf. They needed spatial skills to be able to hit a target from a distance—whether it was an animal that would provide meat for the family or a threatening foe—and they had to be aggressive.

Women stayed home to care for the children and gather berries and roots for nourishment until the men brought home the meat and fish. They needed to communicate with their offspring, to do many things at a time, to remember everything their families needed. Distinct gender roles became the norm. Men were breadwinners; women cared for their families.

Today, our expectations are different. We want our boys and girls to have choices.

> *No matter how adults try to influence our children, girls will play house . . . and boys will race around fighting imaginary foes, building and destroying, and seeking new thrills.*
>
> *—LOUANN BRIZENDINE,* The Male Brain

In today's early childhood classrooms, boys can have tea parties and girls can play ball. But are boys and girls interested in the same activities? Or are boys still more likely to zoom cars around the floor or compete with their friends to be "king of the hill"? And are the girls happier to fill plates with plastic food and dress up like princesses or ballerinas?

In our classrooms, we notice other differences. Many of our boys do not seem to follow directions as well as girls. They wriggle and poke each other when we want them to sit still. They seem to misbehave more often than girls, too. We shrug it off, saying, "That's the way boys are!" and we are right. According to Louann Brizendine, MD, author of *The Male Brain,* scientists used to think gender differences resulted solely from socialization. Now we know that many of these differences are wired into our brains. Nature plays a significant role. Many of the characteristics and behaviors teachers find troubling are predetermined by the male brain.

How Boys' Brains Work

The following information applies generally to the brains of boys and girls. It is important to remember that all children—boys and girls—are individuals and have their own special mix and degree of gender characteristics.

For years, scientists believed male and female brains were alike and, therefore, boys learned and could be taught in the same way as girls. New scientific technologies such as SPECT, MRI, and PET scans have drastically changed scientific understanding about the roles of "nature" and "nurture" in the development of young children. These technologies show clear structural and functional differences in specific areas of male and female brains that affect learning in profound ways.

The chromosomes X and Y determine the sex of a fetus (XX defines females; XY differentiates males). But male and female brains actually start out the same. According to Brizendine, boys' and girls' brains are identical until eight weeks into fetal development. Then, she says, everything changes. The boy's Y chromosome activates the hormone testosterone, which drenches his brain. The testosterone turns on special genes that trigger characteristics such as the urge to track and chase moving objects, hit targets, test his own strength, and play at fighting off enemies, much like the hunter of ancient times. Later in gestation, the hormone MIS (Müllerian inhibiting substance) completes the transformation and continues to fuel his male-specific brain circuits until he is 10 years old.

When a brain gains a new set of abilities—by forming new or reinforcing existing neural pathways—it "makes room" by pruning unused pathways. For example, when a boy gains male-specific characteristics such as spatial-mechanical abilities, the language centers of his brain lose cells and decrease in size. Girls retain the full capacity of their language centers, which explains why girls' verbal skills are generally superior.

Left Brain, Right Brain

The brain is divided into two halves, referred to as the *left brain* and the *right brain*. You have undoubtedly heard creative people referred to as "left-brained" and methodical types as "right-brained," but that is only part of the story.

The left side of the brain has the primary responsibility for verbal abilities and information processing (abilities such as speaking, reading, and writing), which are generally stronger in girls. The right side houses the centers for visual information, spatial relations, patterns, and abstract thinking (abilities more often associated with boys). Each side of the brain controls the opposite side of the body. So your brain's left side controls your right hand, for example, and vice versa. Damage to one side of the brain affects the other side of the body.

Without getting too specific, it is important to know that the verbal centers in the male brain are split between the right and left hemispheres, making it more difficult for boys to retrieve verbal information. In girls, the verbal centers of the brain are located only in the left section. The opposite is true for the visual-spatial centers. In boys, they are located strictly in the right hemisphere; whereas, in girls, they are split between the two hemispheres. This makes the visual-spatial pathway for boys quicker and more efficient.

The left and right sides of the brain are connected by a thick strand of nerves called the *corpus callosum*. Here girls have an advantage: their corpus callosum is thicker, meaning they have more connections between the hemispheres, so more information can be exchanged from one side to the other. This benefits girls in terms of integrating information from throughout the brain. Girls are able to do more things at the same time. Some scientists have even speculated that this is the reason for women's superior intuition. The male brain, in contrast, is more focused.

The hemispheres and corpus callosum also play a role in the emotional responses of males and females. Male emotions stem from the brain's right side, and males have fewer connections to the left side's verbal centers, which makes it more difficult for them to express their feelings with words.

Sections of the Brain

Within the brain, several sections play roles in further differentiating males from females. They include

- the *brain stem*—controls basic body functions;
- the *midbrain*—controls motor activity;
- the *cerebellum*—coordinates movement and balance;
- the *limbic system*—controls emotions, attachment, and memory; and
- the *cortex*—controls thinking, reasoning, language, and decision making.

To put it simply, the midbrain and cerebellum, which are involved in functions such as motor activity and movement, are more active in boys; girls have the advantage in areas involving emotions, memory, and language. That makes sense with what we know about the genders, but it is much more complicated than that.

Each subsection of the brain has its own specific functions. Take a look at this representation of the brain.

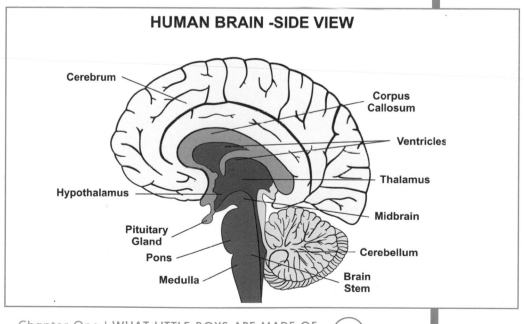

HUMAN BRAIN - SIDE VIEW

Cerebrum
Corpus Callosum
Ventricles
Thalamus
Hypothalamus
Midbrain
Pituitary Gland
Pons
Cerebellum
Medulla
Brain Stem

The brain is built from the bottom up. The lowest part of the brain, including the brain stem, midbrain, and cerebellum, is the most primitive. It evolved hundreds of millions of years ago and controls basic bodily functions such as heartbeat, respiration, digestion, and movement as well as instincts for survival, mating, and dominance.

The limbic system, sometimes called the emotional brain, is next, having evolved around 150 million years ago. This section controls emotion, memory, and behavior; it includes the amygdala, hippocampus, hypothalamus, pituitary gland, and thalamus.

The cortex is the last section of the brain to have evolved, and this is primarily what separates humans from other beings. This top portion of the brain controls functions such as thinking, reasoning, and decision making. It contains 80 percent of the brain's neurons and continues to develop through and beyond adolescence. It is not fully developed until age 25. Among its subsections are the frontal lobe, parietal lobe, temporal lobe, occipital lobe, and corpus callosum.

When we look at brain scans, we find that some sections of the brain are more active in males and others in females. Males and females also have different proportions of white and gray matter in their brains. In Table 1.1, you will see the brain sections that tend to "light up" more in male and female brains, respectively, and the functions they represent.

Table 1.1

MAJOR MALE/FEMALE BRAIN DIFFERENCES		
Section	Function	More Active in
Brain stem	Physical responses	Male
Cerebellum	Physical action, "doing"	Male
Amygdala	Aggressive responses	Male
Cerebral cortex	Judgment, impulse control, attention	Female
Limbic system	Emotion, bonding	Female
Temporal lobes	Speaking, listening, reading	Female
Left hemisphere	Verbal	Female
Right hemisphere	Spatial/mechanical	Male
Parietal lobe	Spatial processing, tracking	Male
Corpus callosum	Cross-talk between hemispheres	Female
Basal ganglia system	Sense of calm, well-being	Female
Hippocampus	Memory	Female
Gray matter	Project focus	Male
White matter	Multitasking	Female
Occipital lobe	Vision	Male

Adapted from Daniel Amen, "A Brain Science Approach," and Michael Gurian, *Boys and Girls Learn Differently.*

The Effect of Hormones

Much of the behavior of boys and girls (and men and women) is driven by hormones. Hormones turn on (or off) genes that are linked to specific kinds of male and female behavior.

We have talked about the way a boy's brain changes in the fetus when testosterone first floods his brain. Testosterone continues to be the dominant hormone in boys. It fosters male physical characteristics, aggressive tendencies, territoriality, and, later on, sex drive. It tends to make boys competitive, always striving to be "king of the hill." It creates more brain circuits for exploratory behavior and rough-and-tumble muscle movement. As they grow older, males with high levels of testosterone tend to be more aggressive, have larger muscles, and be more dominating and ambitious. Those with lower levels are likely to be more sensitive, more mild mannered, and less athletic.

The hormone MIS (Müllerian-inhibiting substance) also has a role in forming the brain circuits that spur exploratory behavior, muscle and motor control, spatial skills, and roughhousing. [7]

The hormones vasopressin and cortisol combine with testosterone to stimulate boys to physical action when their "turf" is challenged. These hormones also make boys more prone to taking risks.

Females also have some testosterone and can have some of these qualities to a lesser extent, but their dominant hormones are estrogen and progesterone, which foster female physical growth, aid in bonding and attachment, and incline girls to cooperation as opposed to competition.

Two other hormones—oxytocin and serotonin—also play important roles in the differences we see in boys and girls. Both are more active in females. Oxytocin plays an important role in reproduction, pair bonding, anxiety, and maternal behavior. Although its main function is to aid female reproduction, it also helps young girls

7   Brizendine, Louann. 2010. *The Male Brain*. New York: Broadway Books.

develop empathy. Serotonin is called the "feel-good" chemical; it is not processed as well in boys' brains, which tends to make boys more impulsive and fidgety.

Nature and Nurture

Information on how boys' brains are structured helps us better understand their natures. We need to remember, though, that many other factors contribute to a boy's development: his family, his environment, his culture, and, of course, the teachers who guide his learning. The early brain is just a starting point.

We also need to understand that boys and girls have these tendencies to greater or lesser degrees. For example, girls have some testosterone, and boys have some estrogen. They are individuals first, each with a brain and hormones in a special mix.

These findings do not mean that either gender is more intelligent; boys and girls just use their brains differently.

Why This Matters to Early Childhood Teachers

Many early childhood teachers instinctively know they need to deal with boys and girls differently. But now we have concrete evidence of the unique structure and function of boys' and girls' brains—evidence that points to new ways teachers can help boys perform at their best.

Generations ago, children learned from their families. Many boys—even very young boys—worked on the farm, learned skills, and hunted and fished with their fathers. They engaged in physical pursuits. The things they learned were more in tune with their natural tendencies.

Now fathers usually work outside the home. Boys learn from women—their mothers and the mostly female teachers in their early childhood classrooms—whose brains are more verbally oriented. So it is not surprising that there is often a mismatch. In learning about boys' brains, we have discovered how much our classrooms are geared to the ways girls learn. Girls happily sit and listen. Boys' brains are geared to activity and movement.

There is increasing evidence that these differences are at the root of many of the problems boys are having in our early childhood classrooms. We see far too many boys classified as having behavior problems. We see far too many boys falling behind academically. And we see that far too many of these boys are African American or Hispanic/Latino.

The good news is that there are ways we can improve the behavior and the performance of boys in the classroom, whether their teachers are female or male. We simply need to adapt teaching methods to the ways boys learn best, and we need to ensure that male perspectives and role models are present and integrated into classroom activities.

In our Boys' Project, results show that modifying our classrooms and teaching methods to address gender differences can make a difference. This has proven invaluable in advancing boys' learning and improving classroom behavior.

As teachers of our youngest children, we know how critical these early years are to a child's development and to a child's later success in school and in life. This is the period when children's brains grow synapses, soak up knowledge, and create the building blocks for future learning. Now we also know that nature has given boys brain characteristics that are uniquely theirs, to be treasured and enhanced in a special way. We need to use that knowledge to create classrooms that work for boys and for girls. When boys do better, girls do, too.

NURTURING BOYS' BRAINS

Chapter 2

Facts and Strategies for Early Childhood Teachers

Now that we know boys' brains work differently than girls', how do we use that knowledge in our early learning classrooms? We spent a lot of time considering this and enlisting the help of experts both in Cleveland and around the country. Then, we translated this knowledge into simple strategies our teachers could use in their classrooms. Finally, we tested these strategies in pilot classrooms, and now we want to share them.

> School is where you sit all day and the women talk.
> —A young boy,
> in Helping Boys Succeed in School,
> Terry Neu and Rich Weinfeld

In this chapter, you will find the brain-based facts and strategies we have found to be most appropriate and helpful for nurturing boys from three to six years old. In later chapters, you will find sections that address the unique needs of the many young African American and Hispanic/Latino boys shown to be the most at risk. We will also address other issues—environmental, cultural, and teacher/family—that have an effect on the development of young boys.

The facts, guidelines, and strategies included in this book are meant to enhance the ways you work with the boys in your classroom and are in no way intended to minimize attention to girls. We also want to reinforce the message that boys themselves differ from one another. Accommodating different characteristics helps in the healthy development of all children in a classroom.

Boys Are Wired to Move (Not Sit Still)

It does not take brain science to tell us that boys tend to be in perpetual motion. Whenever they have the chance, they run, chase, and race. They zoom cars, dig in sand piles, and build forts. On their own, you will rarely find them sitting quietly and listening. Boys are naturally wired for movement.

It is a process that begins in the womb with the megadoses of male hormones—testosterone and MIS—that shape and differentiate the male brain, predisposing boys to be more physical than girls. Boys have larger muscles, even when they are young.

Nearly all the brain centers involving physical activity—such as the brain stem and cerebellum—are significantly more active in boys. More of a boy's blood flow is processed in the cerebellum, which controls physical action.

When boys move—even if they are just twisting, turning, or squirming—their brains wake up. Boys react physically to everything around them. Their muscles and nervous systems appear to be involved even when they think, read, and speak. When a boy learns the word *run*, for example, his leg muscles twitch—as if he is rehearsing the action to learn the word.[8]

When a boy is physically active, his brain is active. When he is inactive, so is most of his brain. A boy's brain is geared to recharge itself between tasks. If his brain is not stimulated, it tunes out and lapses into a neural rest state, shut down by as much as 70 percent. (In contrast, 90 percent of the female brain tends to remain active.) When this happens, a boy will often do whatever he can to keep his brain awake. If a reading circle goes on too long, he might lie down on the floor and roll, bump shoulders with the child next to him, or hit another child's arm to get a reaction. Boys are less able than girls to sit and listen for long periods of time. Their attention spans and learning abilities are tied directly to movement and activity.

Boys tend to get bored when they are not moving; they get fidgety, and they do not pay attention. This can create problems in early childhood classrooms. Remember that boys need stimulation to keep their less-active brains awake.

Boys also do not have the same ability as girls to calm themselves down. This is because of their basal ganglia and the fact that they do not have as much oxytocin in their system. Nor do they have as much ability to process serotonin, which tends to make them more fidgety. All of these impulses can cause problems if teachers expect boys to stay very still for a long time. Boys can learn when they are sitting. Just let them squeeze a ball or tap their feet.

---

8   Brizendine. *The Male Brain*, 26.

Generally speaking, the key to engaging boys is keeping them physically active. Boys need time and space to move around and expend their boundless energy throughout the day. When they are moving, their brains are alert.

What to Do

■ Find ways for boys to move during sitting or standing times. During group times, include activities that allow boys to move—play games, act out characters in stories, find opportunities to stand, or jump or march to music. For example, if you are reading *Click, Clack Moo: Cows That Type,* break to let the children act like cows. If they are standing in line, let them march in place, raise their hands, or engage in other physical activity.

■ Schedule "brain breaks." If you see a boy wriggling or poking a neighbor while you are reading a book or engaged in another quiet activity, that is your cue to get him—and the group—up and moving. Plug in "brain breaks"; for example, stretching or 60-second movement breaks such as jumping to keep boys' brains active.

■ Provide squeeze balls or other handheld items that boys can manipulate to keep them engaged during "listening" times.

■ Alternate quiet and physical activities to keep boys engaged.

■ Put boys to work during group times. Give them jobs that require movement during circle or group activities; for example, posting items on a board.

■ Increase outdoor and indoor large-muscle activities. Schedule plenty of time for outdoor play, and make sure you have sufficient space and play equipment. When outdoor play is not possible, try to find large indoor spaces in your building or a room at a nearby church, recreation center, or other facility.

Boys Excel at Spatial and Mechanical Tasks

Why are so many boys good at games where they catch or kick balls? Studies show it is because of their spatial ability. The biggest difference between the brains of boys and girls is boys' ability to picture three-dimensional objects in space—not just their shapes but their positions, too. Boys also have an advantage in eye-hand coordination.

These abilities are rooted in the fact that boys are generally more right-brained than girls. Their parietal lobes give them superior spatial processing skills, and their retinas have cells (M ganglion) that allow them to better see objects that move around them. You can see this from birth. Male babies like to look at mobiles and other objects that move in space. Preschool-age boys like to build things with blocks, play with cars and trucks, and manipulate anything that moves, spins, or rolls. They can construct complex structures, often building them up until they tumble. In contrast, you will usually find girls building lower, more horizontal structures.

Boys have an innate ability to visualize, manipulate, and track objects in space and make mental rotation. They can imagine how objects might look when turned around in three-dimensional space; they can follow the trajectory of a football or a baseball as it moves through space and then position their bodies to catch it. This and their superior eye-hand coordination give them an advantage in ball-oriented sports.

These are a boy's most pronounced natural abilities—and boys need opportunities to develop them and gain the confidence that comes from doing things well. It is also important to help girls develop the spatial/mechanical skills that do not come as

KEEPING BOYS ON THE MOVE

We make sure boys get enough movement to keep their brains engaged throughout the day. During circle time, we play active, fun games. When we read books, the children love to act out some of the characters. When changing activity centers, they are encouraged to stomp and "silly walk," which makes them laugh and smile—and accept directions more easily!

The boys in our Maple Heights Family Life Child Care Center, who are mainly African American, love to have us put on Super Fun Show CDs of Afrocentric music so they can move to the beat.

The right mix of small- and large-group music and movement activities is incorporated into our daily plans.

naturally to them—the same way we want to help boys improve their verbal abilities.

What to Do

- Have enough blocks and building materials. Most classrooms have blocks—block building is very important for boys—but classrooms often lack enough blocks or other materials to create the complex structures that preschool boys are capable of building. Research tells us boys can use 300–400 blocks in a single building project, so we suggest stocking at least 500 blocks. Consider adding different kinds of blocks that permit more complex structures. The same concept applies to LEGO bricks and other building materials.

- Allow enough space for building activities. Make sure your block area is spacious and away from the flow of traffic to prevent the accidental toppling of structures.

- Include large building materials for group projects. Develop group projects where boys (and girls) work together to create large, complex structures—forts, garages, or barns—and have them bring in cars/trucks or animals, if they wish, to mirror a physical environment. This enhances spatial abilities, manipulation, and balance and connects the child to the real world, which aids learning.

- Offer indoor and outdoor activities where boys can manipulate objects. Have different sizes and types of balls, and encourage outdoor ball-handling activities, games, and free play. Indoors, stimulate these abilities with opportunities to manipulate boats, water, pails, shovels, and sand.

LOTS MORE BLOCKS!

In our pilot Boys' Project programs, we have greatly expanded the space for building with blocks as well as the number and kinds of blocks (size, shape, material) available. Among the new favorites in the Lakewood Family Life Child Care Center are blocks in geometric shapes that boys can fit together to make all kinds of designs. (The girls like them, too.)

A TOWERING PROJECT

Boys like to build complex structures—the higher, the better. Christie Stemplinski, a teacher at Small Hands Big Dreams Learning Center in Bainbridge, Ohio, shares an idea for a group project that "just happened" and got her boys more excited and involved. Her girls enjoyed it, too.

I was watching a group of boys make towers in the block space. When the towers reached a certain height, they collapsed. At one of the tables, a group of girls was making collages with different kinds of paper, glue, and glue brushes.

After a while, one girl, Isabella, asked, "Can we have something big to glue?" So we started working on group collages, adding more items. On the table, we placed a variety of items—corks, buttons, sticks—in containers so the children could pick out what they wanted to use. I brought the groups together. They found that corks served as excellent blocks, and became excited to see how many corks they could stack.

Then one of the boys, Ty, asked, "Why can't I get these to go any higher?" So we began to study how we could make higher structures. The children noticed that when they put two towers together, they supported each other and did not fall down. With this in mind, we built a three-dimensional collage and kept adding to it.

Next, they wanted to build a tower that reached the ceiling!
We started collecting boxes, tubes, and more and more boxes! Every day we added two or three more objects to our tower. Before we began, we had to decide which boxes to place next. This taught the children about sizes—which were bigger; which were smaller? Groups of four applied thick layers of glue to one side and on top, then placed the boxes.

Our interest grew as quickly as our tower! Building it has given us unique opportunities to explore different concepts of measurement. How tall is the tower? How tall are we? Are we taller than the tower? One day we went to the office to get a "measure stick." We measured our tower, and then each of the children compared the results. How many people are the same height? Who is the tallest? Who is the shortest?

We found a wonderful way to learn together, nourish our brains, and gain a sense of accomplishment.

Boys Develop Verbal Abilities Later Than Girls

We know that girls usually talk earlier and have better language skills than boys. Studies confirm this. Boys speak their first words later than girls, and their speech does not become 99-percent comprehensible until they are four years old, a full year later than girls. A preschool girl has a larger vocabulary, has better grammar, and forms longer sentences than a boy of the same age.

That happens for good reason. As discussed earlier, boys lose cells in the verbal centers of their brains when testosterone enters their systems in the womb. The brain's left-hemisphere speech center develops earlier in girls and is more efficient. A girl's temporal lobes—which help in the understanding, processing, and retrieval of language—are also more active.

Because of their natural predilection toward language, girls rely on words to express themselves more than boys, not only in the early years but also throughout their lives. Boys are more likely to use silent cues.

This can be a problem in our early classrooms because we rely mainly on words to communicate—and communicating with boys at this age can be difficult. Because our culture relies so heavily on words, we need to help boys close the gap as early as possible.

Among the ways to stimulate boys' verbal abilities is to develop strategies that take their natural tendencies into consideration. They learn better when more senses are involved, especially vision and touch—when they move, and when they see or hear about things that interest them.

For example, we know that boys relate to things that move or growl or fly. Reading books about trucks or animals or planes is one way to spur boys' interest and verbal skills. They respond to pictures and like to make sounds and move like animals and planes. Incorporating these elements is a great way to get their language skills moving, too.

What to Do

- Keep verbal instructions to less than a minute. This makes it easier for boys to process what you say.
- Nurture boys' and girls' verbal abilities differently. Recognize that gender differences exist in acquiring verbal skills, and teach the boys and girls differently. This allows you to give special attention to bringing boys up to speed while also nurturing girls' earlier verbal abilities.
- Show pictures and let boys manipulate objects. Adding visual aids and manipulatives to lessons helps boys learn at the same pace as girls.
- Stimulate verbal abilities with books that appeal to boys. Preschool boys are interested in real-life books and stories filled with excitement and action. Have lots of these kinds of books visible throughout the classroom, and read them often:
  - Books on real-life people, places, and things, and how things work and grow
  - Stories about boys, animals, cars, trucks, and construction, as well as funny and action-oriented stories
  - Books on superheroes, cultural heroes (pioneers, founders, scientists, inventors), and everyday heroes (firemen, policemen, servicemen/women)
  - Books with pictures of animals, dinosaurs, sea creatures, bugs, spiders, and snakes.
  You will find a list of recommended books for boys in the Resources section of this book.
- Bring fathers and other males into the classroom to read books. Sometimes boys think reading is a "girl" thing. Bringing adult males into the classroom to read to the children shows that men value reading, too.
- Use music to stimulate boys' verbal abilities. Music is a "whole-brain" activity that uses both the left and right brain

hemispheres. It helps all children learn, soothes emotions, and gives boys the special benefits of improving their verbal abilities by linking words to music. Evidence shows that background music can help boys learn and adds a soothing presence.

- Sing or make up songs that relate to a subject you are discussing.
- Dance to music rhythms.
- Play musical games.
- Introduce simple instruments and have children march to the beat.
- Keep a library of different kinds of music and play music at the start of the day to accompany activities, for games, and for relaxation.

- Have boys act out stories. This spikes their interest and adds the physical movement boys crave.
- Place boys on your right (as you face them) during circle time or other times when you are speaking to them. This way, the information is more likely to go into their right ear, then to their brain's left hemisphere.
- Give boys encouragement. Make sure to give them extra praise and lots of high fives when they do well in anything—from following directions to learning activities. Praise them when they have done something positive, telling them specifically what it was they did to earn the praise; tell them how special they are.

Nationally boys are scoring lower in reading and in writing than girls, and their lead over girls in areas like science and math has now virtually disappeared.

—*TERRY NEU AND RICH WEINFELD*, Helping Boys Succeed in School

Shortly after we began our Boys' Project, we started a Read2Me program to bring male readers into our classrooms throughout northeastern Ohio. We have recruited retired teachers, businessmen, shop owners, high school and college students, and other volunteers to read books to the children in our early childhood classrooms. This shows the boys that men value reading—that it is not just for girls.

Our volunteers know the connection between movement and boys' brains—so you will often see them acting out stories and having the boys join in. In one of our classrooms, we were surprised to see a prominent businessman waving his arms, pretending to be flying, with the children joining in, while he read a book about planes.

Boys Learn by Doing (Rather Than Listening)

We have talked about boys' need to move and their innate ability to manipulate objects. It is not surprising, then, that boys are hands-on learners. They learn best by moving, climbing, touching, building, and taking things apart. Boys learn by doing.
When boys have the opportunity to manipulate things—puzzles, blocks, LEGO bricks, TinkerToys, or stringing beads, for example—they are not only developing their fine and gross motor skills but also activating their brains, figuring out how things work, and triggering their learning abilities. They even learn their letters and numbers better through hands-on activities.

As noted earlier, males are born with better spatial and mechanical aptitudes, while females have the advantage in speech and verbal abilities. Girls also listen better and have a longer attention span. According to neuroscientist Daniel Amen, that is because females have more neural activity in the frontal and temporal lobes—the brain's primary listening and language centers. Males have a smaller density of neurons in these areas, according to Godfrey Pearlson of Yale University. They do not pick up as much of what is said to them. Boys also have less oxytocin and fewer verbal mechanisms in the brain, so they do not take to learning as easily or as well as girls when they are sitting and talking.

For boys to learn at their best, they need an action-oriented approach—they need to be physically, as well as mentally, engaged. When we add sensory/tactile experiences, we help boys' brains soak up learning. Studies also show that girls benefit when more senses are involved—75 percent of all learners and an even higher percentage of boys retain more if they learn this way. So, it is good for everyone!

What to Do

- Have toys and puzzles that children can pull apart and reassemble. Offer hands-on opportunities for children to figure out how to put things together.
- Teach ABCs through manipulation and movement. Boys will remember their ABCs and numbers more easily if you find creative ways, such as the following, to incorporate manipulation and movement in your teaching:
  - Use arms and legs to make letters (the YMCA approach).
  - Make letters and numbers out of clay.
  - Play a game where you hide the letters of boys' first names and give the boys oral clues to find the letters; then, ask the boys to organize them.
  - Play a Twister-like game where children connect letters using their bodies.
  - Teach numbers using touchable familiar classroom objects.
  - Count the plates needed to set the lunch table; then, set the table.
- Sort play vehicles into groups (cars, trucks, farm equipment) and count the number in each group.
  - Teach simple addition using coins, vehicles, or other objects. Add one group to another to come up with the answers. The same approach can be used to teach subtraction.
  - Teach about bones, muscles, and so on through movement activities such as the "Hokey-Pokey." Here is a hint from *Sesame Street*: Talk about what muscles

and bones do, and have children feel them in their bodies. Then dance the "Hokey-Pokey," changing the words to "Put your hand bones in." "Put your knee bones in." "Put your toe bones in." "Put your leg muscles in." "Put your stomach muscles in." "Put your shoulder muscles in."

- Encourage boys to create artwork to aid learning. When boys draw or create artwork, they are moving and stimulating their brains. Have boys create artwork—collages, coloring, and so on—from a story you have read. Have them make up their own stories and draw or paste simple pictures to illustrate them; have them find and paste photos of insects, animals, and dinosaurs you are learning about. They will remember a story or lesson better because their spatial and visual centers are involved. Verbal improvement often follows.

Boys are programmed to move, make things move and watch things move.

—LOUANN BRIZENDINE,
The Male Brain

Boys Need Lots of Space

There is no question that boys need a lot of space—much more than girls. Boys not only need to move more than girls; they normally are also physically larger and take up more space. Three-year-old boys have more muscle mass than girls of the same age. They run more. They have more interest in exploring the physical world around them. Their spatial/mechanical brains are geared to building, racing, throwing and catching, and taking things apart, spreading them out, and putting them back together. Whether they are working at tables, playing with blocks, or out on the playground, boys simply need their space. In contrast, girls relate to their surroundings more through the verbal centers of their brains and are happy to play in smaller spaces.

When they are inside, boys sometimes seem like bulls in china shops. They can be in everyone's way—using the classroom floor as their personal monster-truck track, running when they should walk, and spreading blocks out so no room is available for anyone else to play. When they do not have enough space, boys often get frustrated, which can end up in arguments and behavior problems. That can lead teachers to think boys are being inconsiderate when they are simply testing their brains and exercising their natural tendencies.

While boys do need to obey classroom rules, changing something as simple as the amount of space they are allotted can alleviate behavior problems, keep territorial disputes to a minimum, and help boys avoid the temptation to touch, bump, or punch one another, which often happens when they are too close together.

What to Do

- Allow more elbow room during group activities. Instead of crowding children together for circle time and other group activities, have them sit or stand farther apart.
- Limit the number of children in each activity area. Keep a small group of children in each activity area so that each one has the needed space. For example, instead of having five children in a LEGO area, try keeping the number to four.
- Limit the number of children at tables. Most early childhood classrooms have tables that accommodate eight children. Consider allowing only four children at a time at each table, and space the children apart.

A SPECIAL PLACE FOR EACH CHILD

*During circle time in Maple Heights Family Life Child Care Center's pilot Boys'
Program, you will not find children pushing or crowding together to grab a spot near
the teacher. When Miss Naomi tells them it is time, the 10 children in the class head
quietly to sit down in their own special places, marked with duct-tape letters that
spell out their names.*

*Miss Naomi has the space arranged in a semicircle. She is in the middle. Each child's
space has plenty of room around it—not just to avoid being distracted by a neighbor
but also because Miss Naomi adds a lot of movement to her stories and lessons.
On this day, she is reading about Saint Patrick and how he drove the snakes out of
Ireland. She points to a picture. "What color is that?" she asks. Several children say*
verde. *(She is also teaching them words in three languages besides English.) Soon she
has them up on their feet, pointing to the green in the clothes they are wearing and
marching in place like they do in the Saint Patrick's Day Parade. Later they will get
their instruments and march around the room, having their own parade before
settling down to a tasty, nutritious lunch
that has lots of green vegetables and a
green dessert they made themselves.*

FINDING ENOUGH SPACE

The Family Life Child Care Center in Lakewood, Ohio, is in an older home with limited space and well-defined play, eating, and naptime areas. Finding the space boys need was difficult there, but Lakewood's teachers were up to the challenge. They moved their activity areas around, setting up a large area in the front of the house for dramatic play. One side has the child-sized kitchen, table, and chairs; the other side has costumes, gear of all kinds, and space—for pretending to be superheroes, ballerinas, policemen, firemen, musicians, doctors, and nurses. (So it is no longer just a "housekeeping" area.)

When a group's free-time activities are in the dramatic play area, the children—both boys and girls—often make a beeline for the Power Ranger costumes, in which they will pretend-rescue kittens or each other from imaginary harm. But soon, they are likely to move on. You will see a boy putting on a fireman's hat, a girl with a doctor's jacket over her pink Hello Kitty shirt and a stethoscope in her hand, and a small group in the kitchen area acting out a family scene—eating dinner, coming home from work, or going off to school—giving a good balance.

Outdoors, the center has made the most of its space and budget, adding to the playground equipment with an ABC dinosaur, hopscotch, and other games painted on the pavement by a local Girl Scout troop.

The Maple Heights Family Life Child Care Center is housed in a church. In addition to a large outdoor play area, the boys have opportunities to develop large motor skills indoors in the church's large gym. Here they play pretend basketball; engage in physically active, fun play; and are encouraged to invent their own games.

Boys Are Geared to Do One Thing at a Time

Boys are at their best when they can focus on a single task at a time, and girls are better at multitasking, for several reasons. Males have 6.5 times more gray matter than females—which makes their brains more adept at processing information locally in one part of the brain. Females have about 10 times more white brain matter, which helps them process information from many parts of the brain simultaneously. Their corpus callosum also is up to 25 percent larger, giving them more "cross-talk" between their left- and right-brain hemispheres.

A boy's advantage in gray matter gives him the ability to concentrate on complex tasks at an early age. He is likely to become absorbed in an activity and want to complete it before moving on. It can be difficult to tear him away. The tendency to focus on one thing at a time can make it difficult for a young boy to understand more than one instruction at a time. This "task focus" also can cause a boy's brain to become overstimulated when he is asked to process several things at once, adding to the difficulty.

If a preschool teacher asks a boy to (1) complete an activity, (2) put materials away, and (3) find another interest area—all in one sentence—the boy will need to juggle several directions simultaneously; in other words, he must multitask. Both the teacher and the boy can become frustrated when the boy does not seem to be following directions.

As teachers, we need to realize that we cannot expect boys to do several things at a time. They simply are not made that way. What we can do is nurture their capacity for complex projects and give directions in ways that improve their chances of success.

What to Do
- Let boys stay with activities longer. Instead of moving them from one activity to another in a set 15- or 20-minute time period, as many teachers do, allow boys to stay with an activity as long as they are engaged. For example, if a boy

is deeply involved in block building, give him the option of continuing instead of moving to another activity.

- Use a different approach to multistep directions. Usually, a boy will remember the last in a series of steps or the instruction that sticks in his mind. When you want to give a boy instructions, you need to first get his attention away from what he is doing. Try using this technique:

    - Place your hand firmly on his shoulder or arm, giving slightly more than the light touch you would give a girl.
    - Once you touch him, he will likely look at you. That may be your best opportunity to make natural eye contact.
    - Give him the first direction, and ask him to repeat it. For example, say, "I want you to put on your coat. Now, what is it that I want you to do?" Listen as he repeats your directions. Then ask him one more time, "What do I want you to do?" Listen again as he repeats your directions.
    - Wait until he has completed the first task to give him the second direction, repeating the above steps. Do the same with additional directions.

Boys Need Time to Make Transitions

You will probably agree that moving children, especially boys, from one activity to another is one of a teacher's most difficult and time-consuming tasks. For all small children, transitions are important times when they need to prepare themselves for new activities. For boys, this can be especially stressful.

Boys need more time to make changes than girls. Part of the reason is the male brain's tendency to be single-focused, as noted earlier. When boys are invested in a project, they do not want to leave and may not pay attention to the teacher's request.

The female brain has greater blood flow to the anterior cingulate gyrus, the brain's "gear shifter" that runs lengthwise through the deep parts of the frontal lobe and shifts attention from task to task or idea to idea. That gives females the ability to make transitions more easily.

When boys are asked to change quickly, they can get frustrated—their amygdala can swell, causing anger and aggression, and their cortisol and adrenaline levels can increase—which, in turn, can lead to discipline problems.

Boys need plenty of time to get used to the idea that they need to make a transition. They also need clear step-by-step instructions to alert them to what they need to do.

What to Do

- Give plenty of warning. Even for a simple instruction, boys need at least 60 seconds to make a change. A better idea is this: if you expect boys to make a transition in 5 minutes, warn them 10 minutes ahead of time. Let them know when 5 minutes is up, tell them they have 5 minutes left, and so on. (Make sure the times you give are accurate so the children trust them.)
- Use sounds or music as cues. Consider using different sounds or musical pieces to signal different activities. A favorite song could be played as a cue for circle time; a drumbeat might alert the children that it is time to go outdoors.
- Give instructions one at a time. Much the same as in the last section, you need to first get the boys' attention, then give each direction separately. A boy may remember only one instruction, so start with the first one. When he completes that task, give him the second, and so on. For example, start with "We are going outside. Please put your toys away." Walk away, then return and instruct the boy to get his coat, and ask him to repeat what you said. Once that is complete, repeat the process with the next instruction—in this case, to get in line to go outside. It will take a teacher no longer to do this than to redirect those boys who show up in line without their coats or who put on their coats and do not remember what they are to do next.

As time passes, try giving the children two directions simultaneously, again asking them to repeat each instruction after you.

At our Lakewood Family Life Child Care Center pilot Boys' Program, Miss Michelle often uses a timer when she is getting the children ready to move from one activity to another. Andrew is eager to put on a Power Ranger costume in the dramatic play area, and he continues to pester her about moving. She touches his arm (because boys respond best to physical communication), looks him right in the eye (gaining his full attention), and tells him and the other children she is setting the timer for 10 minutes, giving them advance warning that they will need to clean up and get ready to move. She repeats the instruction twice more.

Andrew stops pestering her and picks up the magnifying glass that makes his eye look huge and shows his giant eye to another boy. Everyone has time to process the instruction and get ready to move on. Miss Michelle reminds them again when they have 5 minutes, and again at 2 minutes. When the timer rings, Andrew knows it is his turn to be a Power Ranger, and he and the others move smoothly to their next activity.

Boys Are Visual Learners

A boy's eyes are one of his best learning aids. Vision is by far a boy's best sense and his best-developed way of acquiring information. While many children learn their lessons more readily when pictures are added to the mix, this is especially true for boys who rely on the visual more than other senses.

Boys see still and moving objects better than girls. They also have a better sense of perspective. This is due to the M ganglion cells in their retinas. In contrast, girls' retinas have P ganglion cells that are better suited to detecting fine detail.

Boys also see bright colors best. They like them better, too. You will often hear them say that bright reds, blues, and greens are "boy" colors and pinks and lavenders are "girl" colors. Sometimes they will reject toys they would ordinarily play with, such as cars, if they are in a "girl color"! Boys can have difficulty distinguishing lighter colors; they also are more prone to color blindness.

Not just bright colors are important to boys. Boys perform better in bright light. Low light can affect serotonin levels in their brains, making learning more difficult. In winter, having enough light in the classroom is especially important for boys.

Some studies show that boys have a narrower field of vision but a greater focus on depth, while girls see the "bigger picture" because of their better peripheral vision. Girls also see better in the dark.

Boys may have superior vision, but they need intense colors and bright light to do their best. They learn through their eyes, so adding pictures and visual cues will enhance their ability to learn words and acquire verbal skills and will aid retention.

What to Do

- Use primary colors. Wherever possible, use bright colors in wall displays, other materials, and painting and drawing materials for boys.
- Use pictures to reinforce learning. Post and show pictures of people, animals, fruits, vegetables, and other things the boys are learning about. Have them cut photos/drawings out of magazines for a hands-on experience. Post charts and posters with pictures as well as words. Display pictures the boys have made of their families, people they admire, and things that are important to them. Place billboards where boys can reach them and organize their own materials.
- Enhance classroom lighting. Add brighter bulbs, lamps, or other lighting units to boost the amount of light available. Replace extinguished light bulbs. Some

studies suggest fluorescent or screw-in bulbs with a color temperature of 4,000 kelvins are best for promoting boys' learning. In winter, good lighting is especially important.

- Move tables closer to windows. Chances are boys will do better when they are working on projects at tables near windows that let sunlight in the room.
- Arrange rooms so boys are close to visual aids—and be sure visual aids are large enough to be seen clearly.

Boys Are Louder but Do Not Hear as Well as Girls

Boys see better than girls, but they do not hear as well. There is a biological reason—once again, the emergence of testosterone in the male fetus. This makes the male auditory system more focused, limiting much of the background noise as well as softer and repetitious sounds.

In their early years, boys hear better through their right ears, while girls hear equally with both ears and are more sensitive to sound. Scientists think girls hear sound twice as loud as boys do. Their ears are more sensitive to softer sounds and tone of voice. That may be why boys seem to have a higher tolerance for loud noises; they also localize sounds better and have better auditory memories.

If you wonder why you will often hear boys noisily roaring like lions or whining like airplanes out on the playground, they have the ability to detect animal noises and loud sounds better than girls—but girls, beginning in infancy, are better at hearing what people say.

According to research, that is one more reason why young girls surpass boys in verbal and reading skills. Not only do their left-brain hemispheres develop earlier, but girls' ability to hear a family member or teacher speak to them is stronger. Boys are more likely to ignore voices and hear less of what is said to them at this age.

Because boys see better than they hear, some scientists suggest that their reliance on visual processing actually works against their ability to listen to the teacher and learn lessons.

What to Do

- Make certain you can be heard. For boys to hear and understand what you are saying, you will need to speak very clearly and slightly more loudly than you would need to for girls. This is especially important when you are giving instructions or reading a book.

- Keep boys near the front at circle and group times. Make sure boys hear what you are saying by keeping them close. Because they hear better with their right ears, consider placing them to your right as you face them.

- Keep directions short and simple. Because boys do not always hear or process everything you are saying, be direct when you speak to them, keep instructions short and simple, and have boys repeat them after you.

- Reinforce verbal instructions and lessons with visual cues. Because boys pick things up quicker visually, try to have visual cues to help them learn and understand instructions—try using pictures, photos, and symbols to reinforce what you are saying.

Boys Look at Things; Girls Look at People

Just days after they are born, boys and girls already focus on different things.

Girls tend to look at faces and maintain eye contact longer than boys. Boys are more likely to look at mobiles or other moving objects. It does not seem to matter what you put in front of them. When they are just two to four days old, girls spend twice as much time looking at adults who are talking to them. Later on, girls gurgle at people. Boys "talk" too, but they are just as happy to make sounds when looking at toys or other objects. They are more interested in seeing the shapes and patterns.

In our early childhood classrooms (and certainly later on in life), we expect boys to look us in the eye, but this does not come naturally to them. When people, especially strangers, force a preschool boy—or any boy for that matter—to make eye contact, he may run, fight, or stare at them with that "deer in the headlights" look. His brain may be processing the look as aggressive, which increases his level of the neurotransmitter cortisol. This chemical, produced by the adrenal glands, is involved in the fight-or-flight reaction.

If a boy responds this way, he is not processing anything you are saying to him. You need to get his attention in another way. You do not want to startle him first by staring him in the eye. Eye contact needs to feel natural, not forced.

What to Do

- Start with a light touch. If you want to get a boy's attention, touch him lightly on the arm or the back, then look him in the eye, and he will be more likely to respond and pay attention to what you are saying.
- Stimulate eye contact. Try to get boys used to looking you in the eye. When you have a boy's attention or when you are listening or speaking to him, look him in the eye. You already have his attention, so he is not likely to feel threatened. Chances are he will gradually become comfortable, and you will likely stimulate him to follow your example.
- Understand that boys can pay attention without making eye contact. Even if he is not looking you in the eye, a boy may still be processing what you are saying to him. So, even though you want to encourage him to make eye contact, do not be too concerned if that does not come naturally to him.

Boys Remember "Just the Facts"

Boys' and girls' memories work differently. The hippocampus, located in the brain's deep limbic system (DLS), is where memories are stored and is smaller in boys than girls. Boys tend to remember "just the facts." Girls have the capacity to store more irrelevant and random information. They also connect emotional experiences to their memories.

The amygdala functions in a different way in males and females, too. Boys use the right portion, which is associated with action, not emotion. Girls use the left portion, which stimulates emotional reactions; they store their memories by emotional strength and are better at picking up social cues.

A boy looks for patterns, much like his younger self looked at objects instead of faces. Thanks to his natural right-brained spatial/mechanical tendencies, he is better at remembering logical sequences, while his sister has greater ability to remember names and faces.

Boys often need more time to memorize than girls, especially anything related to words. As noted earlier, boys also have a hard time remembering more than one thing at a time. They do better when information is organized in some form, in charts and lists. They also remember information better if it relates to the things they are interested in—if a truck is an F-150 or a Dodge Ram and if a dinosaur is a *T. rex* or a stegosaurus.

What to Do

- Give boys time to memorize. It is a good idea to repeat things you want boys to remember and give them extra time. Girls may be quicker to pick things up, but when a boy does remember something, it will stick in his head.
- Use charts or lists. Have charts or lists of things to do or remember posted around the room using symbols or photos. As an example, a chart showing the children's daily duties might have a photo by each child's name and a picture or symbol showing what each is supposed to do.
- Reinforce lessons and instructions with visual aids. Boys will remember much more if photos or visuals, especially objects or things that interest them, such as vehicles, animals, or insects, accompany lessons. (Girls will, too.)

Boys Bond through Physical Play

Give a boy a high five! Like all of the children in your classroom, boys need to bond—or attach—to the important people in their lives if they are to grow and learn at their best. When they do not do so, they become stressed. When a child is stressed, cortisol builds up in the brain—slowing neural action and activating the brain stem and amygdala, the brain centers that stimulate anger and the fight-or-flight response. At that point, all learning stops. For young boys who are already behind girls in language development, further delays occur. *Attachment stress* can also make boys more aggressive and cause behavior problems.

Boys attach to others much differently than girls. They like high fives better than hugs; they prefer physical play—such as wrestling and roughhousing—to words and facial expressions. We call this *aggressive attachment,* and it is critical for boys, especially preschool boys.

Scientists have found hormones and male-specific neurons that seem to be linked to roughhousing and other typical male behaviors. Boys wrestle and roughhouse up to six times more often than girls. They push their physical limits. This gives them a huge "high"—a rewarding rush of dopamine that makes them want more.

When boys are wrestling around on the ground, you will find they are usually laughing and giggling. This type of play rarely turns ugly, and it is actually beneficial. Boys need plenty of opportunities during the day for games and activities that involve bodily contact and vigorous rough-and-tumble play. It is their way of connecting to others.

What to Do

- Let boys get physical. Make sure you allow enough free time for boys to play physical and rough-and-tumble games and activities, both indoors and out.
- Create an indoor "little gym." Create an indoor space with mats and equipment for physical play. This is especially important in colder climates where boys cannot always play outside. If space is limited, find a place for mats in a corner of the room. Girls also enjoy the chance to practice somersaults and other gymnastics.
- Set rules. Make sure you have rules for physical play, and communicate them clearly. For example, no more than two at a time can wrestle with one another, and they must do so on the mats provided.

- Supervise activity. Keep close watch on roughhousing to make sure it does not get out of hand. If it does, defuse and redirect the energy with a touch or other slight physical action.

- Encourage fathers of children in your classroom—who rarely need encouragement—to engage in rough-and-tumble play with their sons. There is no question that boys benefit tremendously from engaging in physical play with the significant males in their lives.

Boys Are Naturally Aggressive and Competitive

Males are naturally aggressive. Historically, they needed to defend their turf and hunt animals for food. If we compare the brains of males and females, we can see how these traits have lingered—and we understand why the boys in our classrooms tend to be more aggressive than the girls.

In males, the cerebellum, brain stem, and amygdala are more active than they are in females. These areas of the brain control physical responses, action, and aggressiveness, respectively. In addition, males secrete testosterone, which, as discussed earlier, fosters aggression, and vasopressin, which stimulates territoriality and hierarchy. The effect? Males are less calm, less communicative, and more prone to fight aggressively over territory and bond with a smaller network of people. They are very competitive, often striving to be at the very top of the hierarchy. Preschool boys are six times more likely to use domestic items such as spatulas as swords or weapons than as kitchen utensils. Studies show boys spend 65 percent of their time in competitive games compared to 35 percent of girls' time. Girls also take turns 20 times often more than boys.

In females, the brain's cerebral cortex—which manages judgment and empathy—is more active. Girls' dominant brain chemicals are estrogen, progesterone, oxytocin, and serotonin. The effect? Females tend to be calmer, less physically aggressive, less competitive, and more cooperative. They make eye contact, pick up on social/emotional/contextual cues, and bond with a broader network of people.

One important facet of self-control is the ability to express strong emotions in socially acceptable ways. When a conflict occurs, teachers often ask children to talk about their emotions and use their words. That works better for girls. Girls use words to express their feelings. When the brain's amygdala is stimulated by emotional experience, it orchestrates an outward response. In girls, this response comes from the language centers. A boy's response comes from more primitive areas of the brain—the brain stem and cerebellum—so he tends to use his body to express displeasure.

For example, when a girl is angry, the limbic area of her brain signals for a response from the language center. So girls naturally have something to say. Boys process anger in the limbic area, too—but the signal goes, instead, to their brain stem and cerebellum. When a boy gets angry, yelling "Use your words!" probably will not work. He will use his hands before he even hears that instruction. His first response is to use his body—and that can mean hitting or kicking. What is more, when boys respond physically, they get a dopamine jolt from the brain's reward centers.

What to Do

- Intervene quickly when a boy gets angry. Defuse his angry energy, and then talk to him about using his words. Tell him what he can say when he is upset, and say it for him with an angry intonation. For example, "I don't like it when you knock my block house down!" Later, when the stakes are not as high, read books that show appropriate ways to express anger.

Remember, it will take longer for boys to learn this behavior. They will learn it best through repetition—getting it right, getting it wrong, and getting it right again.

- Have an "angry place" where boys can go to release frustration. Redirect angry responses—hitting, punching, or kicking—from animate to inanimate objects. Teach boys to go to a special place where they can get rid of their anger by banging a Nerf bat at a cushion, for example.

- Make sure boys have plenty of vigorous, competitive activity. Preschool boys need outlets for their endless "boy energy." Giving them healthy opportunities to compete in games and children's sports can channel aggressive tendencies.

- Give boys opportunities for physical contact. Nurture healthy aggression with contact games and shoulder-to-shoulder rather than eye-to-eye contact. Make sure the boys understand this kind of physical contact is fine with boys but not with girls.

- Do not take away outdoor time as a punishment. Find other ways to discipline boys. Punishing them by taking away outdoor time can cause boys to become even more aggressive.

- Observe behaviors that cause boys to become aggressive toward others. Try to find out what specific things cause each boy in your classroom to become aggressive; this will help you anticipate, discuss, and redirect inappropriate behavior before it gets out of hand. The same goes for girls who may be verbally aggressive.

- Increase empathy. Show and have children discuss the effect their aggressive actions have on others and the effect others' actions have on them. Read books that offer the same message.

Boys Are Risk Takers

Why does that boy keep trying to jump off the top of the gym? We complain that boys are impetuous and take unnecessary risks. "He acts before he thinks about whether he is making a good choice." Well, there is a reason for that. Some of the same brain characteristics that predispose boys to be physically active and aggressive also make them prone to impulsiveness and risk taking.

The frontal lobe of the brain helps us make good choices in view of the consequences, but note that in both males and females, it does not fully develop until age 25. Girls' frontal lobes are more active and grow earlier than boys'—so girls are more likely to think before they act. A boy's prefrontal cortex is not as active. His brain makes him likely to react regardless of the consequences.

If a boy decides to climb to the highest point of a particular playground structure and jump off, he is not likely to think about safety or what you have said to him about this kind of risky behavior. Even if you tell him not to do it, he will probably find ways to persist when you are not looking or not around. He is getting the same dopamine high that rewards him when he gets physical. This "high" can also cause him to repeat risky behavior.

Because boys are impulsive risk takers, it is essential to set up learning environments to minimize any chance of injury. While we want to encourage boys to explore their environments, we want to reduce risky behavior, and we need to keep them safe.

What to Do

- Ensure safe indoor and outdoor environments. First and foremost, check your indoor and outdoor spaces to make them as safe as possible to limit any chance of injury.
- Monitor and support boys' efforts to explore safely. Let boys use their natural abilities to explore, but do so safely. Watch them closely, especially when they are outside. If a boy is about to take an unsafe risk such as jumping from a high place, redirect him by showing him a safer jumping spot or by helping him jump down safely. After a while, he will grow tired of it, find something more stimulating, and move on to that.
- Give boys choices. For any preschooler, making choices aids brain development and judgment. For boys this is especially important because the brain mechanisms that help them think things through before acting are not as active at this age as they are in girls. So be sure to give them plenty of

opportunities to make choices throughout the day (see Tables 2.1 and 2.2).

Table 2.1 HELPING BOYS IN THE EARLY CHILDHOOD CLASSROOM	
Boys' Brain Tendencies	**Classroom Strategies**
Spatial/Mechanical Abilities	■ Larger workspaces
	■ More blocks, construction materials
Less Verbal Ability	■ Learning through manipulation, movement
	■ Reinforce learning with displays, posters, charts, videos, games, musical activities
	■ Read books about heroes, animals, and boys like them
Movement	■ Indoor and outdoor gym areas
	■ Musical activities
	■ Alternate sedentary and physical activities
	■ Allow some physical bonding
Single Focus	■ Let boys stay with activities they like
	■ Ease into transitions
Good Vision	■ Bright classrooms, colors
Lack of Eye Contact	■ Touch to get attention, maintain eye contact
Memory Issues	■ Repeat directions
	■ Use charts
Aggression	■ Defuse energy
	■ Give specific alternate actions
	■ Read books on proper behavior
Risk Taking	■ Redirect behavior
	■ Make environment safe
	■ Give choices
Inattention	■ Give "brain breaks"

Table 2.2

USING BOY-FRIENDLY STRATEGIES IN DAILY ROUTINES

Boy-Friendly Strategy	How Strategy Is Used in Daily Routine
Boys need more workspace.	■ Tables accommodate eight children; however, limit them to four at a time.
Block play is critical to the learning and development of boys.	■ Expand the block area in the classroom to provide additional space to build large structures. Increase the variety of blocks available (size, shape, material).
Music and movement activities support and promote the learning of boys.	■ Use different types of music throughout the day to extend learning. Incorporate more large- and small-group music and movement activities into daily plan. A Maple Heights classroom favorite is *Super Fun Show* CDs, which include upbeat Afrocentric music that gives all the children an opportunity to move.
Boys need repetition, reminders, and visuals when given an instruction.	■ Implement the three-step approach when giving instructions. Also, consistently ask boys to repeat information to promote follow-through.
Incorporate different types of praise.	■ Give high fives and praise for specific, positive actions, and communicate that children are special throughout the day.
Boys need transition preparation.	■ Ease into transitions, giving plenty of warnings, both verbal and visual. Incorporate a timer.
Directions and transitions that incorporate fun and movement are more effective.	■ Instead of simply telling boys to go to their centers, encourage them to stomp or "silly walk" to their centers. Fun and silly moves make the children laugh and smile and help them with following directions.
Boys like to use their imaginations to create fun and active games.	■ Boys are allowed and encouraged to invent games and play them where appropriate. One example is a pretend form of basketball played in the large motor room. ■ Fun games that the children are involved in creating may also be used during circle time. Boys might make up silly motions for the rest of the children to imitate. ■ Add props and costumes to the classroom, such as capes, helmets, goggles, and trucks, to inspire imagination and positive interaction. ■ A dramatic play center can be developed to be more than just "housekeeping."

Table 2.2 (continued)

USING BOY-FRIENDLY STRATEGIES IN DAILY ROUTINES

Boy-Friendly Strategy	How Strategy Is Used in Daily Routine
Boys need physical interaction and activity to keep their brains going.	■ When boys are observed engaging in physical interaction with one another that is safe and appropriate, acknowledge and allow it.
Boys need lots of light to keep their minds active and engaged.	■ Move centers in the classrooms closer to windows and natural light.
Family-member participation and involvement is critical for success.	■ Hold monthly family meetings at each site. Provide daily notes for parents and other caregivers. Hold a variety of parent-child, and specifically father-child, activities at each site at least quarterly. For example, the Children's Museum came to the Lakewood site for a father-child activity. Also, at each site, hold a cookout or an ice cream social event. Specifically boy-friendly information is provided to families, such as a "Helping Boys Do Their Best" note card. ■ Ask families to help make prop donations to contribute to the classroom.
Diversity is celebrated.	■ At each site, have posters of different male role models from a variety of racial and ethnic backgrounds. ■ Incorporate different languages and types of food into lessons.
Boys respond to the use of superheroes in the classroom.	■ Incorporate superheroes into dramatic play, art and storytelling activities, table manipulatives, and the block area.

RESOURCES USED IN THIS CHAPTER

Amen, Daniel. http://www.amenclinics.com/clinics/professionals/how-we-can-help/brain-science. "A Brain Science Approach," accessed October 2, 2011

Brizendine, Louann. 2010. *The Male Brain*. New York: Broadway Books.

Griffin, Larry. 2010. Notes to author, April 19 (Unpublished).

Gurian, Michael. 2005. *The Minds of Boys: Saving Our Sons from Falling Behind in School and Life*. San Francisco: Jossey-Bass.

Gurian, Michael, and Kathy Stevens. 2011. *Boys and Girls Learn Differently: A Guide for Teachers and Parents*. San Francisco: Jossey-Bass.

Hanlin, Mary Frances, Sande Milton, and Pamela Phelps. 2001. "Young Children's Block Construction Activities: Findings from 3 Years of Observation." *Journal of Early Intervention* 24(3): 224-237.

James, Abigail Norfleet. 2007. *Teaching the Male Brain: How Boys Think, Feel, and Learn in School*. Thousand Oaks, CA: Corwin Press.

Kindlon, Dan, and Michael Thompson. 2000. *Raising Cain: Protecting the Emotional Life of Boys*. New York: Ballantine.

Moir, Anne, and David Jessel. 1992. *Brain Sex: The Real Difference between Men and Women*. New York: Dell Publishing.

Neu, Terry, and Rich Weinfeld. 2007. *Helping Boys Succeed in School: A Practical Guide for Parents and Teachers*. Waco, TX: Prufrock Press.

Schaeffer, Laura. "The Male Brain Explained," accessed October 20, 2011. http://lifestyle.msn.com/relationships/articlematch.aspx?cp-documentid=886075 (article removed from site).

NURTURING AFRICAN AMERICAN BOYS

AFRICAN AMERICAN BOYS: THE STRUGGLE CONTINUES

by Anthony President

Far too many of today's African American boys are in crisis.

Although African Americans have made huge strides, many of our boys still are falling behind. Since the passage of the 1964 Civil Rights Act, advances for African Americans in access to education, upward social mobility through employment, and election to public office have greatly improved. According to the U.S. Census Bureau, over the last 50 years, the high school graduation rates of African American males have more than quadrupled. Many are reaping the benefits of free and open competition for education and jobs.

Others, however, continue to struggle. For them, the struggle begins at an early age. According to the U.S. Department of Health and Human Services, 38.2 percent of African American children under the age of six live in poverty, compared to 30.2 percent in 2001—the highest level since 1993.[9]

Investment in the early years, before age 6, pays the greatest social dividends of all education spending. This is especially true for children who grow up with economic disadvantages.
—David Broder, "Cutbacks to Our Children," The Washington Post

9   ASPE Office of Human Services Policy. 2011. "Information on Poverty and Income Statistics: A Summary of 2011 Current Population Survey Data," September 13, accessed July 17, 2012. http://aspe.hhs.gov/poverty/11/ib.shtml.

THE CRISIS IN AFRICAN AMERICAN EDUCATION

- *African American students are 60 times more likely to be expelled than white students.*
- *In 2005–2006, more than half of black males dropped out of high school, compared with 39 percent of black females.*
- *At the end of high school, 37 percent of black males score "below basic" in writing skills, compared to 17 percent of black females.*
- *Of eighth-grade African Americans, 91 percent are below proficiency in math.*
- *Fewer than 8 percent of African American men are college graduates, compared with 17 percent of white men and 35 percent of Asian men.*
- *Only 7 percent of U.S. teachers are African American.*
- *Black students are more likely to be taught by inexperienced white teachers.*

> *–CARALEE ADAMS, "The Challenge of Teaching across Race," Instructor magazine, February 2008*

Chapman, et al. *Trends in High School Dropouts and Completion Rates in the United States, 1972–2009.*

The Promise and the Challenge

While African American boys of today represent promise, daunting challenges occur along the way. Promise shows when African American boys start off their school careers with positive experiences in early childhood programs—a key factor in setting the stage for positive engagement from grade school through senior high school. Young boys who "buy in" to education can grow up to fulfill their promise of future excellence through positive contributions to society. Engaged boys can become astronauts (Bernard Harris Jr.), doctors (Ben Carson), or even president of the United States (Barack Obama).

Conversely, boys who disengage or do not see themselves as belonging in school or the community present challenges; they can form a negative identity. This negative identity can begin early, between the ages of three and six years, and is characterized by boys who embrace the beliefs espoused in gangsta rap music; negative street culture, film, and television entertainment; and violent or crime-oriented video games. This is most pervasive in low-income urban neighborhoods and in single-parent families with no positive male presence. Young boys can begin early to understand masculinity as skewed toward hypermasculinity.

In the construct of hypermasculinity, young boys see a very limited conception of masculinity, defined by violence and aggression and with "street knowledge" valued over formal education. Rather than developing emotional intelligence, conflict resolution, and problem-solving skills, these boys see models of older boys and men who hit, fight, and commit crimes or yell and curse to achieve their ends and resolve differences.

Likewise, formal education is looked down upon as uncool, unmanly, and white. A real or true man to these boys is one who lives up to these negative values and "keeps it real." As they continue on to school, boys may find themselves mimicking these behaviors to prove to other boys that they are real men. Boys who do not conform to this standard may find themselves bullied, ostracized, and friendless. Young boys may dumb themselves down and act out to fit in and be accepted. This fosters a youth culture whose values are contrary to academic achievement, peace, and good citizenship.

Boys naturally wish to emulate the older boys and men around them. These visible examples are reinforced by bad media images of African Americans. Young boys are bombarded with negative images and beliefs on a daily basis through the music heard in their homes, the music videos seen on TV and the Internet, and the actions modeled by older boys and men in the community. If boys see it both in their neighborhoods and on TV, they conclude it must be true. A negative identity seems their only option.

According to research by the late Dr. George Gerbner, television has been the predominant storyteller for children instead of parents, for over 30 years. On a daily basis, the stories told by media reinforce the negative identity.

Harvard sociology professor Orlando Patterson, in the March 26, 2006, *New York Times* article "A Poverty of the Mind," reports that sociologists have identified a "cool pose" culture of young black men that devalues education and promotes negative street culture. This cool pose is mimicked by boys who look to emulate the behaviors of their older brothers, cousins, and neighbors in the community.

According to Patterson, youth find the "cool pose" culture immensely gratifying and believe that it is all there is. Negative hip-hop culture that promotes the "cool pose" lifestyle is pervasive and ever present in the video and computer games and media used by both young boys and their older brothers and kin. Often, both young boys and older boys play and participate in the media together, where the older boys teach the younger.

Attitudes toward Education

What happens when boys get older and go to school? In his classic work *Countering the Conspiracy to Destroy Black Boys*, Dr. Jawanza Kunjufu coined the term *fourth-grade failure syndrome*. Kunjufu theorized that the boys who show early promise and potential often become emotionally detached from school by the fourth grade.

This emotional detachment from school is not the result of a change in intellect. So, what might be a plausible cause? Certainly, it could be the boy's attitude about school. Poor attitudes about school translate into poor performance. Poor performance ultimately ends in academic failure, which further opens the door to the boy identifying with negative role models.

Psychologist Erik Erikson theorized that youth who form a negative identity may resort to extreme delinquency in an effort to deal with their failures. This delinquency can occur in the form of crime, violence, drug and alcohol use, or other irresponsible behavior. Boys who remain disengaged may find themselves in the criminal justice system.

THE EFFECT OF NEGATIVE IDENTITY

- *The arrest rate of African American youth ages 10–17 is almost twice that of their white peers.*
- *Almost 60 percent of young inmates serving time in adult prisons are African American, even though African Americans represent only 15 percent of the youth population.*
- *Nationally, one out of every three young African American males is in prison or on probation or parole.*

Before the 1980s, the African American community looked down on serving time. Today, it has become a desirable badge of courage for many. Author and former prison inmate A. Scot Washington asserts, "Serving time in prison has become a sort of rite of passage for many inner-city young persons, both male and female."

Many of today's inner-city youth have grandfathers, fathers, and uncles who have served time in prison. For the first time, it is possible for four generations of a family's men to be in jail, in prison, in juvenile detention, or on probation or parole at the same time. The question we need to ask is "What will be the long-term effect on the preschool boys who witness this today?"

> *African American males have higher unemployment, lower labor force participation, lower high school graduation, and [lower] college enrollment rates while ranking first in incarceration and homicide as a percentage of the population.*
>
> *—MYCHAL WYNN,*
> Empowering African American Males

It is critically important that early childhood educators influence these boys, before these negative beliefs become ingrained, by offering positive male images, bringing good male role models into the classroom, encouraging the participation of fathers, and adopting strategies that are more boy and African American friendly.

African Americans represent an extraordinarily large proportion of boys in crisis.

Anthony President, president of Presidential Consultants, Inc., *is a motivational speaker, a seminar trainer, and the president of Presidential Consultants LLC, a consortium of training professionals who address child welfare and other issues. He is a certified trainer of the Institute for Human Services and a college instructor. He has long dedicated himself to making a difference.*

Mr. President believes that understanding the environment boys grow in is the first step toward setting them on the path to a positive life.

Facts and Strategies
for Early Childhood Teachers

The boys in our early childhood classrooms come from a variety of cultures, neighborhoods, and life experiences. They do not always fit neatly into the mainstream. Some face the daily challenges of poverty and crime-ridden neighborhoods. Some come from families torn apart by drug addiction and alcoholism. Many young African American boys are at risk, as the statistics attest. They need special attention, especially those from inner-city neighborhoods or single-parent homes. Starting them out on the right track early is crucial to keeping them motivated, in school and beyond. And early childhood is the place to begin.

> *We must commit ourselves to doing whatever it takes to ensure that the most vulnerable students in our education system receive the support they need to thrive.*
>
> —ROSA A. SMITH,
> *"Saving Minority Boys"*
> *eforum, www.renniecenter.org.*

All the boy-friendly strategies we discussed earlier work regardless of racial background. The following are additional and specific to boys who are at risk. It is important to stress that a great many African American boys of today are doing well—succeeding in school and going on to successful careers. The following strategies are for those boys whose futures look bleak unless we intervene in their early years and start them on the path to a healthy, productive life.

Develop Relationships with Boys, Their Families, and Their Neighbors

When a three-year-old boy enters your classroom, he brings with him the sum of his early experience—much of which he has learned at home and in his neighborhood. By getting to know the boy and the people around him, you will get a keen sense of what matters to him, what family strengths may have been passed on, and whether any problems might impede his learning—knowledge that will be invaluable in understanding the best ways to reach and teach him.

What to Do

- Arrange a home visit. Visiting a boy's home before he begins school may be the best clue to helping him achieve in your classroom. You will meet his family and observe the dynamics that have helped shape his early years:
    - What are the family's hopes and dreams?
    - What positive/negative influences surround the child?
    - What do family members like to do—listen to music, read, watch TV, play video games, play sports?
    - Who are the family's heroes?
    - Are any family issues affecting the child?
    - Who is the child's primary caregiver?
    - What does the family believe are the child's strengths, and in what areas would the family like to see improvement?
    - What are the education levels of members of the family?
    - Will the family members support and participate in your programs?
    - Do any positive male role models live in the household?
    - What are the family's values?

  Keep an open mind, and do not approach the family unit with any preconceived biases or assumptions. When making the home visit, be genuine and show interest.

- Bond with the boys in your classroom. Find out about each boy's personality, learning style, interests, and abilities, and areas where he may need to improve. Work to develop a strong relationship. Shake hands or high-five the boys when they come into the classroom. Touch their shoulder or back when they participate in class, give a good answer, or do something special. Show interest in their lives. Remember that little things mean a lot.

- Make friends in the neighborhood. Find out about the neighborhood each boy lives in and develop relationships with churches, social services, programs, and businesses that can provide mentors, activities, and services that can enhance the lives of each boy and his family.[10] You will get valuable information from them, and they may be able to help with your early childhood programs.

---

10 Kuykendall, Crystal. 1991. *From Rage to Hope: Strategies for Reclaiming Black and Hispanic Students*. Bloomington, IN: Solution Tree.

Focus on Strengths, Not Problems

Like everyone else, African American boys have hosts of natural abilities—abilities that blossom with the right care and attention. Unfortunately, these boys are not always given the chance, particularly in low-income urban environments. Sometimes, the street culture holds them back. Other times, boys have difficulty acclimating to the predominantly white culture. They might face overwhelming problems at home. Or, they are simply misunderstood.

Another factor is at play, too—many young boys have a deep fear of authority figures such as policemen—and this fear can extend to teachers.

Youngsters with these fears often become stressed out, have trouble learning, or aggressively act out their issues and are identified as behavior problems. When they act this way, it is easy to see only the negatives. In his book *Teaching, Parenting, and Mentoring Successful Black Males*, Mychal Wynn suggests a constructive alternative. If we expect boys to flourish, he says, we need to "look at their gifts, not their deficiencies."

Janice Hale-Benson, a highly regarded author and professor of early childhood education, agrees. In her book *Black Children: Their Roots, Culture, and Learning Styles*, she adds that the best place to begin is by recognizing the strengths of young African American boys and building "bridges between the areas in which they seem to be 'naturally' proficient, such as music," and learning activities.

What to Do
- Be a good coach. Good coaches get the most out of their players. They set high expectations, motivate and respect their players, and put them in the best position to win. Teachers are wise to follow coaches' examples—encouraging, advising, and giving boys opportunities to be successful. Even discipline can be approached in a positive way (see the section "Use Constructive Approaches to Discipline." Coming

down too hard can bring out instinctive fears and make boys withdraw or become aggressive.

- Understand communication styles. African American boys often express themselves with their own creative language, their facial expressions, and their bodies. It can be hard to understand what they mean, which sometimes is the opposite of what they say. They play word games that may sound threatening but really are not. Watch for nonverbal clues in their gestures and eye contact, and do not take everything they say literally. Do encourage them to express themselves in ways that can be understood by everyone.

- Teach to the beat. Rap music is the second greatest influence on African American kids today, even young ones. Chances are they can spout all the words to these songs—and that shows they can memorize, and they can learn. If they are having trouble, teach ABCs and 123s to a rap beat. Help them come up with their own raps to learn colors, names of animals, and other things. Some good educational rap and hip-hop is available, too; for example, *Sesame Street's* "Rappin' Alphabet," "A-B-C Hip Hop," and "Queen Latifah: The Letter O," which can be found on the website Sesamestreet.org; *Super Fun Show* CDs (Superfunshow.com); Hip Hop Harry (Hiphopharry.com); and Alphabet Rockers (Alphabetrockers.com). Jazz, rhythm and blues, and disco are other music forms that should be incorporated into the classroom.

- Channel extra-high energy. Studies show African American boys often have higher energy, motor activity, and testosterone levels than whites. It is important to channel these tendencies early by allowing more time for large-muscle activities and competitive games. These boys' high-octane intensity can be construed as hyperactivity or channeled into athleticism. Testosterone-fueled aggressiveness can be molded into constructive leadership.

- Foster creativity. To see how supercreative African American boys can be—and how they love to express themselves—is easy. Give them plenty of opportunities to make up stories and create artwork that taps into these natural abilities. Do not be concerned if their stories feature lots of action and destruction—that is natural for young boys. In art projects, let them use the bright, bold colors they find stimulating and encouraging and that help their brains develop.

- Team them up. Boys this age love to socialize and do things together—but, at the same time, they are competitive. Pair them up in teams—create contests that tie into learning activities, games, or everyday objectives such as attendance.
- Do not embarrass them in public. These boys can have fragile egos. It is important not to undermine their confidence by making them do things in public that they do not do well. If they are way behind in remembering their ABCs or in reading, do not ask them to recite or read in front of others.

Promote a Positive Racial Identity

Take the time to equip yourself with background information on the African American heritage—and communicate it. Instilling pride in their culture and traditions is important to helping boys learn at their best. This is particularly important if your own background is different.

Many young African American boys associate being smart with acting white—a belief that undermines their self-confidence and their ability to perform well in school, and a belief that is perpetuated by their peers. They need to understand that African Americans have made significant contributions in many areas, not just in sports and entertainment. They need to know that African American males value learning.

What to Do

- Learn and teach children about their racial heritage and culture. Tell them about African American history, culture, art, music, folklore, literature, and foods. Talk about the accomplishments of African Americans and how they overcame difficult obstacles before becoming successful. Instill a sense of pride in who they are and where they are from.
- Give children opportunities to share information about their own heritage, family, and traditions. Have children bring in items from home, such as foods that represent their heritage

and family. Talk about special things their families or friends do on holidays or other special occasions. Ask them to bring in photos—or draw pictures—of their families, trips, outings, or other special things they do or want to do, and post them on boards.

- Create opportunities for boys to learn about the work, family, and community experiences of exemplary African American males. Bring fathers, male relatives of children, and exemplary males from the community into the classroom to talk about their life's work and participate in classroom and outside activities.
- Post pictures and posters of African Americans. It is important for children to see admirable people who look like they do. Make sure the classroom has plenty of pictures or posters of African Americans in different roles, including
    - prominent scientists, authors, artists, inventors, engineers, and government officials (for example, President Barack Obama, George Washington Carver, Dr. Martin Luther King Jr., poet Langston Hughes, Supreme Court Justice Thurgood Marshall, former Secretary of State Gen. Colin Powell, NASA administrator and former astronaut Charles Bolden, Grammy-winning composer and musician Quincy Jones, inventor Garrett Morgan, artist Henry Tanner, Nobel Prize-winning poet and playwright Derek Walcott, author Alex Haley, and physician Ben Carson);
    - African American males working at different professions and occupations (for example, lawyers, doctors, firemen, computer programmers, builders, teachers, and scientists); and
    - the families of children in the program.
- Read and discuss books about African Americans:
    - Use age-appropriate biographies of high-achieving African American males to show how these individuals achieved success—and how they overcame tremendous obstacles. The story of Dr. Ben Carson is an excellent example.
    - Read stories about African American children and their lives, as well as their problems and how they surmounted them.
- Make sure books on African Americans are visible in the classroom. Place books showing African American boys

prominently in the classroom. You will find a librarian-recommended list of these books in the Resources section of this book.

- Celebrate African American holidays and special events. Commemorate occasions such as Kwanzaa, Martin Luther King Day, and Black History Month by telling stories and posting pictures of African American history, traditions, and accomplishments.

- Remember to give the boys high fives and praise when they do something positive, noting specifically what they did.

Note: We have not included sports stars and entertainers in this list—those names are well-known because it is important for boys to recognize the accomplishments of men in less publicized fields. Also, we suggest that classrooms feature not only African American males but also other groups that mirror the ethnicity, race, and gender of children in the class.

> ### A CONSTANT REMINDER
>
> *You will notice the pictures and posters right away when you step inside our Maple Heights Family Life Child Care Center. Highly visible, on the opposite side of the room, is a large display of photos and drawings of families—the children's own families: boys and girls with fathers, mothers, brothers, sisters, grandparents, aunts, uncles, and other people who are special to them. Almost all of them are African American families, reflecting the children in the classroom, making them feel at home, and showing how much their families are valued here.*
>
> *At the front of the room, you will see posters of some of America's most famous, most accomplished African Americans—for example, Martin Luther King Jr., U.S. President Barack Obama, U.S. Supreme Court Justice Thurgood Marshall, and George Washington Carver—giving the children a constant reminder of what they can become and showing them people who look just like they do.*

Involve African American Men in Early Childhood Activities

Having good role models is a key to anyone's success, and it is crucial for these boys. Some have good role models at home or in their neighborhood, but many of these boys do not. In his book *Understanding Black Male Learning Styles*, Jawanza Kunjufu says the three most popular careers for underprivileged African American boys are sports, rap, and drugs. That is what they see and hear about. It is critical to expose them to other possibilities.

In addition, a large number come from female-headed single-parent households lacking positive African American male influences. In their early childhood programs, they also find their teachers are nearly always women.

Boys need adult men to look up to—men who believe in education, men who have benefited from staying engaged in school, and men who are role models in many different fields.

Wherever you can, involve men in your activities—men of all ages, from high-achieving high school students to grandfathers. Exposing boys to men they can emulate is an excellent way to help them value learning.

What to Do

- Hold career days with male guests. Have African American males—businessmen, firemen, police officers, accountants, plumbers, professors, professional athletes—speak to your class on career days. Pull your pool of speakers from parents, professionals, patrolmen, firemen's associations, or community organizations.
- Take your class on field trips. Arrange to visit firehouses, neighborhood businesses, museums, zoos, and other places to interact with men with interesting jobs.
- Recruit male readers. Ask children's grandfathers, fathers, brothers, and male neighbors, as well as male middle school and high school scholars, to read to your preschoolers. This shows that older males value reading and—especially when you bring in male African American teens to read—reinforces the notion that not all older boys embrace a negative identity.
- Hire male teachers and aides. Hire some African American male teachers and aides or recruit volunteers, fathers, and other men to help in the classroom on a regular basis.

- Encourage mentors. Encourage single mothers to make use of mentoring programs where adult males encourage and interact one-on-one with boys and take them on outings. Some ideas are listed in the Resources section under "Child/Parent Support/Mentoring Organizations."
- Make classrooms father friendly. Encourage input and participation from the fathers of African American boys. Host father-son or other events to ensure that fathers or other significant males in the boys' lives participate in activities. Know the first names of the fathers, and greet them warmly when you see them.

BRINGING IN THE CAVS

Cleveland's NBA basketball team, the Cavaliers, sent its mostly African American high-energy Scream Team and mascots, Moondog and Sir CC, to the Maple Heights Family Life Child Care Center to jump-start the Read2Me program. This entertaining crew read books, played games, danced, and talked with the boys, bringing huge smiles to the children's faces and showing them that people care about them—and like to read, too.

Set Expectations High

If the people around African American boys do not believe they can succeed, the boys will not believe it either. In many instances, educators have lowered their standards and expectations to what they perceive are the levels at-risk children can achieve. Consequently, these low expectations influence teacher attitudes and are picked up by the children. A better approach is to set high expectations that stretch children's abilities, help them grow, and build self-confidence.

What to Do

- Learn about, discuss, and support their hopes and dreams. Start them thinking about what they could become when they grow up. What do they like to do? Discuss in simple terms what they would need to do to be successful. Talk about college. Encourage them to follow their hopes and dreams.

- Encourage them to look beyond their surroundings. Show them pictures and read books about people and places far and near; for example, African Americans who explored new parts of the world, came up with inventions, and discovered new ways to do things. Show them possibilities beyond what they see in their neighborhoods. Identify other people they respect—prominent or otherwise—to reinforce your message.

- Expose them to constructive occupations. Many African American boys want to emulate the sports figures and entertainers they see on television. Introduce them to other interesting occupations, and give them a sense of what these people accomplish—doctors healing people and coming up with cures for diseases, lawyers fighting for justice, firefighters saving people from disasters, and so on.

- Encourage them to take initiative and learn about and do new things. Give them opportunities to make choices and suggestions, to explore things that interest them, and to move beyond their comfort zones.

- Encourage them to think for themselves, not follow others. Read stories about and discuss challenges, issues, and obstacles boys face. Ask what they would do in similar circumstances. Let them think about and answer some of their own questions where appropriate. Give them opportunities to make choices.

- Have them set goals. When boys create and achieve their own goals, they learn patience and persistence and gain self-confidence. Have each boy create a small daily or weekly goal. Ask him what steps he needs to take to achieve the goal and what might prevent him from reaching it. Write down each step on a sheet and post. Review it at the end of the day, and adjust accordingly. When he completes a step or reaches a goal, he gets a star or other visual acknowledgment. Because boys are so competitive, this is a fun way boys can compete with themselves and make progress.

- Believe these boys can achieve excellence whatever their circumstances. Whether boys are slow learners, have behavior problems, or are top performers, always believe in them, build on their strengths, and help them overcome their limitations.
- Join with family members to agree on expectations. African American families want the best for their children. They have high aspirations for them, but do not always know how or what to do, or they do not have time. Many are young, single women struggling to survive. Reaching out to them can be difficult. But it is critical to find a way. Boys can be confused if family members and teachers do not agree on expectations. Teachers can offer information and resources to help families expand their horizons.

> *We need to take everything we know about gifted education and children along with our behavior toward gifted children and their parents and apply it to black boys.*
>
> *–ROSA A. SMITH, "Saving Minority Boys" eforum, www.renniecenter.org*

Use Constructive Approaches to Discipline

Boys from difficult home environments often engage in aggressive, attention-getting behavior. When this happens, teachers need to be assertive and redirect boys who are aggressive toward others.

One strategy many teachers use is constructive consequences—a method that rewards boys when they perform well and redirects them when they do poorly. Ken Blanchard, author of *Whale Done! The Power of Positive Relationships,* suggests adopting this approach.

What to Do

Implement a constructive consequences approach. When a boy does something right,

- praise him immediately,
- tell him specifically what he did right or almost right,
- tell him you are pleased/proud/happy with what he did, and
- encourage him to keep up the good work.

When a boy does something wrong,

- tell him right away what he did wrong—clearly, specifically, and without blame;
- show him the negative effect of his behavior;
- if appropriate, take the blame for not making directions clearer;
- tell or ask him what he could have done instead, and make sure he clearly understands;
- tell him you have trust and confidence in him; and
- have him assume personal responsibility for his actions. When a boy does something wrong or hurts another person, discuss it with him and make sure he accepts responsibility for his actions and does not put the blame on others.

RESOURCES USED IN THIS CHAPTER

Adams, Caralee. 2008. "What Are Your Expectations? The Challenge of Teaching Across Race." *Instructor*, 117-118: 26-30.

Blanchard, Ken. 2002. *Whale Done! The Power of Positive Relationships*. New York: The Free Press.

Broder, David S. 2003. "Cutbacks to Our Children." *Washington Post*, March 23.

Chapman, Chris, Jennifer Laird, Nicole Ifill, and Angelina KewelRamani. 2011. *Trends in High School Dropout and Completion Rates in the United States: 1972-2009* (NCES 2012-006). U.S. Department of Education. Washington, DC: National Center for Education Statistics, accessed July 24, 2012. http://nces.ed.gov/pubs2012/2012006.pdf.

Hale-Benson, Janice. 1986. *Black Children: Their Roots, Culture and Learning Styles*. Baltimore: Johns Hopkins University Press.

Hering, Beth. n.d. "Help Boys Get More Out of Elementary Education," accessed June 4, 2011. http://www.volunteerguide.org/hours/service-projects/elementary-education

Kunjufu, Jawanza. 2011. *Understanding Black Male Learning Styles*. Chicago: African American Images.

Kuykendall, Crystal. 1991. *From Rage to Hope: Strategies for Reclaiming Black and Hispanic Students*. Bloomington, IN: Solution Tree.

Patterson, Orlando. 2006. "A Poverty of the Mind." *The New York Times*. March 26,

President, Anthony. 2009. Notes to author, October 5 (Unpublished).

Smith, Rosa A. "Saving Minority Boys," accessed June 11, 2011. http://www.renniecenter.org/eforum/07-02E-forum.html#Smith.

Wynn, Mychal. 2007. *Teaching, Parenting, and Mentoring Successful Black Males: A Quick Guide*. Marietta, GA: Rising Sun Publishing.

Wynn, Mychal. 2008. *Empowering African American Males*. Marietta GA: Rising Sun Publishing.

Chapter

4

THE CULTURAL CHALLENGE FOR HISPANIC/LATINO BOYS

by Felix Muniz, DMin,

Executive Director, Galilean Theological Center

The Hispanic/Latino community is the youngest and fastest-growing segment of the population in the United States. These people come from at least 20 different countries, and see themselves as members of a group. They often call themselves *Hispanics* or

We aren't just individuals, we are each a product of our families. Familia is the very center of Latino culture. It's the strongest thing about us and the most universal.
–Gregory Nava, filmmaker

Latinos. Hispanic/Latino is not a race; it is an ethnic classification made up of individuals with European, Native American, and African ancestry.[11]

11 Cassidy, Rachel C., and Elizabeth C. Grieco. 2001. *Overview of Race and Hispanic Origin.* Washington, D.C.: U.S. Department of Commerce, Economics, and Statistics Administration, U.S. Census Bureau.

Just in the past eight years, the Hispanic/Latino presence has increased by more than 11 million, making them the largest minority group at 47 million strong. According to the U.S. Census Bureau, Hispanics/Latinos will surpass the 132 million mark by 2050, accounting for 30 percent of the total U.S. population. Once limited to the West and Southwest, Florida, New York, and Chicago, Hispanics/Latinos are now found in virtually every part of the United States in growing numbers.

This growing, diverse community brings distinct cultural values and orientations, and these, in turn, present new challenges. The rising number of young Hispanic boys will likely need more developmental screening, prevention, early intervention, and coordination of services. If service providers do not receive the cultural-competency training necessary to respond adequately to the complexity of issues affecting the well-being of Hispanics, then the boys' future, and the community's as well, stands to be adversely affected.

Hispanics/Latinos as Outsiders

Even though Hispanics/Latinos have lived for hundreds of years on the land that eventually became the United States, they are still seen as aliens, exiles, and outsiders—people who are marginalized because they are perceived as not belonging. For U.S. Hispanics/Latinos, it is an experience that permeates their everyday existence.

The worldview of the dominant culture in the United States marginalizes the U.S. Hispanic/Latino community because of the tenor of its racial discourse. Hispanics/Latinos live in a social context where the racial discourse has been reduced to a debate of black versus white.[12] Those outside of these categories have been devalued as "nobodies."[13]

Hispanics/Latinos are neither Latin American nor U.S. American. They are neither black nor white. Yet, just as they are none of these things, they are all of these things. They are perennial "others," always in a state of *otredad* (otherness).

While they all share a common Hispanic culture as part of the colonial heritage and mixture of races and traditions, there are many differences. These differences are, with all their colonial and neocolonial influences, a blessing and a promise. They are affirmations of rich diversity. The interconnection between race and culture as a process of *mestizaje* (a mixture) is a key to understanding who the Hispanics/Latinos are as people.[14]

Hispanic/Latino Core Values

To meet the needs of Hispanics/Latinos, we also must understand the core values of this underserved community. At least five core values exist in the Hispanic/Latino community.

The first one is *personalismo*. In *personalismo*, dignity and respect are derived through the process of socialization. One's uniqueness and self-worth are defined through human interaction. However, for most Hispanics/Latinos, direct confrontation is avoided.

The second core value is *machismo*. *Machismo* is the notion of male dominance. The male is the provider and the protector of the family. The male has the complete decision-making power in the family.

---

12 Goizueta, Roberto S. 1992. "Nosotros: Toward a U.S. Hispanic Anthropology." *Listening: Journal of Religion and Culture* 27(1):55–69.
13 Bañuelas, Arturo J. 1995. *Mestizo Christianity: Theology from the Latino Perspective.* Maryknoll, NY: Orbis Books.
14 Elizondo, Virgilio. 1988. *The Future Is Mestizo: Life Where Cultures Meet.* Bloomington, IN: Meyer-Stone.

This brings us to the third core value, *familismo*. *Familismo* is a strong love for children–in fact, as many as the Lord sends. This implies that sex and family roles are well defined. This involves loyalty, reciprocity, and solidarity. A strong identification and attachment occurs with nuclear and extended families. In fact, for many Hispanics/Latinos, there is no such thing as extended family; there is just family.

The fourth core value is *marianismo*. This is the ideal of the Virgin Mary. It asserts a passive and submissive role for women. It is the idea that women are spiritually superior to men. Hispanic/Latina women see themselves as self-sacrificing, with complete dedication to their husbands.

Last, but not least, is *fatalismo*. As is true of many other minority communities, Hispanics are deeply religious. While most Anglo-European congregations register decline in membership, Hispanic congregations are growing constantly. This development transcends geographical and denominational boundaries, as Catholic, mainline Protestant, and Pentecostal church develop in different parts of the nation. Most Hispanics/Latinos are Roman Catholic. They rely very strongly on fate and divine intervention. Their famous saying, "*Lo que Dios quiera*" (It is God's will), attests to their perspective. This saying also derives from the sense of powerlessness, hopelessness, and inability to control and direct.[15, 16, 17]

To educate Hispanic/Latino boys, teachers need first to understand their culture; second, to help them with language skills; third, to make them feel welcome; fourth, to give them successful Hispanic/Latino role models; and fifth, to employ boy-friendly classroom strategies.

15 Lopez-Baez, Sandra. 1999. "Marianismo." In Jeffrey Scott Mio, Joseph E. Trimble, Patricia Arredondo, Harold E. Cheatham, and David Sue, eds. *Key Words In Multicultural Interventions: A Dictionary*. Westport, CT: Greenwood.

16 Marin, Gerardo, and H.C. Triandis. 1985. "Alloncentrism as an Important Characteristic of Behavior in Latin American and Hispanics." In Diaz-Guerrero, Rogelio, ed. *Cross-Cultural and National Studies in Socal Psychology*. Amsterdam: Elsevier Science Publishers.

17 Santiago-Rivera, Azara L., Patricia Arredondo, Maritza Gallardo-Cooper. 2002. *Counseling Latinos and La Familia: A Practical Guide*. Thousand Oaks, CA: Sage Publications.

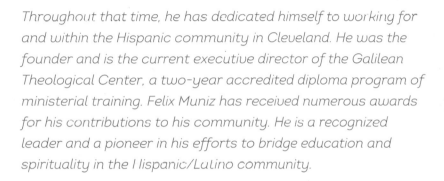

Felix Muniz, a native of Puerto Rico, immigrated to
the United States in 1968. He received an associate's
degree in accounting from Westchester Business
Institute in 1979. Not content, he continued his
education at Ashland University, where he received a
bachelor of arts degree in psychology, and at Ashland
Theological Seminary, where he was awarded a
master's degree in biblical studies and a doctorate of
ministry in Hispanic/Latino theology.

Throughout that time, he has dedicated himself to working for
and within the Hispanic community in Cleveland. He was the
founder and is the current executive director of the Galilean
Theological Center, a two-year accredited diploma program of
ministerial training. Felix Muniz has received numerous awards
for his contributions to his community. He is a recognized
leader and a pioneer in his efforts to bridge education and
spirituality in the Hispanic/Latino community.

Facts and Strategies for Early Childhood Teachers

Boys from Hispanic/Latino families share many of the same
difficulties as urban African American boys, and some of the
same teaching strategies apply. But there also are differences—
some major, some subtle.

Like their African American cohorts, many of these boys
do well, thanks to supportive families and a close-knit
community. Others do little more than exist in poverty-ridden
neighborhoods where teen gangs roam, violence is rampant, and
hopes and dreams are eclipsed by the daily struggle to live.

They see that their culture is not like that of the majority white
population. They are different. Many of their families do not
speak much English, making it difficult to make their needs
known to the outside community or get the good jobs that

can propel them to a better life. Hopelessness fuels the violence they see erupting around them, mostly from older males in the neighborhood.

How can early childhood teachers address the downward spiral that stifles too many young Hispanic/Latino boys? Three main things stand out. We need to

- help them communicate well in English,
- understand and celebrate their culture, and
- establish warm relationships with them and their families.

These underpin all the strategies in the following pages—all are aimed at starting young Hispanic/Latino boys on the right path, whatever their circumstances.

BUILDING CHARACTER

- *Children get their thoughts from parents, teachers, relatives, friends, neighbors, music, movies, television programs, and the Internet.*
- *These thoughts play in their minds, and the children evaluate and consider imitating them.*
- *This leads to attitudes. Attitudes are prepackaged decisions ready to happen.*
- *If the idea looks like it will produce pleasure, they are likely to do it. If it does not, they will probably stay away from it.*
- *The first clues to children's attitudes can be seen in the things they say, their body language, the clothes they wear, and the ways they decorate their space.*
- *The next thing children will do is to take action.*
- *These actions then turn into habits.*
- *The habits become their character.*

Parents and educators need to intervene when poor attitudes start showing up. And they must be persistent. This is critical to the development of healthy children.

—FELIX MUNIZ, DMIN, notes to author, October 5, 2009

Help with English-Language Skills

Once a Hispanic/Latino boy enters school, proficiency in English often determines whether or not he is successful academically. Young children learn new languages quickly, especially if they are exposed to them on a daily basis. Since boys naturally lag behind girls in verbal abilities, it is especially important that they acquire English-language skills before they enter school.

What to Do

■ Find out in advance if the child speaks English. If the child does not speak English well, be sure to have an aide or a teacher in the classroom who speaks his language. Learn to recognize and speak some words in Spanish yourself. Remember that many variations of Spanish exist. Mexican Americans speak differently than Puerto Ricans. It is best to make sure your Spanish-speaking associate comes from the same culture. The same principles apply to children who speak languages other than Spanish.

■ Assess his English proficiency. Determine how well the boy can speak English, if at all. Most young boys have had some exposure to English—through television, older siblings, or children in the neighborhood—but may not speak it well or process the language adequately. To help a boy improve his English-speaking ability, you need to find out how much he knows. Begin with your own observations—how well does the boy listen, understand, and speak? Watch his reactions to what you are saying, and listen carefully to the way he expresses himself. Observe the way he interacts with the other children. To get a more thorough view, it is advisable to bring in outside professionals trained in conducting these assessments. Proficiency instruments are also available.

- Help him build English skills. The results of the assessments will guide you, and many resources are available to help. Young children are quick to learn new languages. Just being in a classroom where English is spoken will be helpful.

- Enlist other children to help. Have the children in the classroom tell him the English words for objects in the different activity areas as they are playing. This will not only help him with his English but also will help him bond with the other children. In return, he can teach the children the same words in Spanish— so all are learning.

- Model standard American English in the classroom, with correct grammar, complete sentences, and correct pronunciation, paying particular attention to "ing" and "th" sounds.

- Encourage the child to keep up his Spanish-language skills. Children find it easy to use mostly English once they become proficient, as the language is used all around them; but, being bilingual is to their advantage. Knowing more than one language advances their skills in both languages and opens up more options as they grow older.

Learn about Hispanic/Latino Culture

Children learn what to say, how to behave, and what to value from their culture—and teachers work best with them by understanding their culture. Even if they have been in the United States for a while, studies have shown that families are still influenced by their ancestors' cultures after five or six generations.

The Hispanic/Latino culture has many variations. Spanish-speaking families come from Mexico; Puerto Rico, Cuba, and other Caribbean islands; countries in Central and South America; and Spain. Some were born there; others were born here. Some like to be called Hispanics; others prefer to be known as Latinos. Each of these groups differs somewhat in language and culture.

Other differences exist, too. Some may be citizens or legal residents; some may be migrant farmers who are here temporarily; others may be here illegally. To teach the children well, teachers need to understand each unique situation.

The more teachers know, the easier their jobs become, and the better the children progress.

What to Do

- Examine your own beliefs and attitudes. If you are not Hispanic/Latino yourself, think about what you believe about Hispanic/Latino culture. Contrast that with what you know about it. Eliminate stereotypes, and set out to discover the reality.

- Learn about Hispanic/Latino history and culture. Read about overall Hispanic/Latino history, geography, accomplishments, and culture to get a basic understanding. See the Resources section in the back of this book for suggestions.

- Learn about specific Hispanic/Latino cultural groups. Find out which countries or islands the boys' families emigrated from, and learn about the customs, traditions, food, art, and music. Knowing this information will help you relate well to the boys and their families. Plus, it will give you ideas for teaching about their cultures, decorating the classroom, and celebrating special occasions.

- Get to know the neighborhood. Visit the neighborhoods the boys live in, and meet some of the people. Observe and drop in to Hispanic/Latino agencies, community centers, grocery stores, churches, and social service organizations. They can give you valuable insights and may even provide resources for the boys or your classroom.

- Learn some Spanish words. If you do not speak Spanish, learn some common words and phrases in the language—and teach some to the children in your classroom.

- Be culturally sensitive. Understand, accept, and appreciate their culture. Do not look at it through the eyes of your own background or assume one is right and one is wrong.

Connect with Boys' Families

In the Hispanic/Latino culture, the family unit is very close and includes not only the mother and father but also grandparents, aunts, uncles, and other family members. Extended families play a larger role than in the typical American family. Teachers, ministers, and counselors are not just individuals who do things for the family; they, too, are part of the family.

The family is always first in the Hispanic/Latino culture, followed by the community, church, and ethnic group. The parents generally are affectionate and nurturing; they teach their children to be cooperative. They give and expect loyalty. In traditional homes, fathers are dominant; mothers are submissive.

As their son's teacher, you are, to them, part of their super-extended family.

What to Do

- Arrange a home visit before the children begin school. A home visit is the best way to begin a relationship with the family. A sure-to-be-appreciated gesture would be to bring them a personal gift—such as a plate of freshly baked cookies. If they offer food or a beverage, be sure to accept.

If you do not speak Spanish well enough to communicate with the family, bring someone along who can translate. Keep an open mind, and do not approach the family unit with any preconceived biases or assumptions. When making the home visit, express genuine interest. Make sure the members of the family know you are there to help their son. Look at displayed photos of the family. Observe, and engage in small talk, but do not appear to pry.

Try to ascertain

- where the family is from and how long the family members have been in the United States;
- what the family's beliefs, values, traditions, and needs are;
- how the family members have assimilated into American life;
- how much English the family members know;
- what the family members' strengths are;
- what the family members' education, employment, and income situations are;
- what the family members' hopes and goals are for their child;
- what the family's perceptions of the boy's strengths and areas needing improvement are; and
- what obstacles, in the family's view, might stand in the way of the boy's learning.

Assuming they have visited your classroom and know about your program, tell them how you hope to work with them and how they can participate—and encourage them to do so.

- Agree on expectations. Work with families to develop common expectations for their sons. Make sure they know that consistency at home and in the early childhood program is key to the children's progress. Hispanic/Latino parents and other family members expect their children to do better than they have; they need to know this is important. When families and the early childhood teacher can agree on the goals for a child, family members are more likely to participate. When they cooperate, the child benefits.

- Keep in close contact. Keep families abreast of what the children are learning, how their sons are doing, and any areas of concern. Ask family members for their input. Face-to-face communication is the best approach, even if that means having a translator present. If that is not possible, call the family members. Give them information on what the children are learning and on activities in which parents can participate. Remember that these parents tend to be interested in activities that help their children academically and socially, not fund-raising.

  It is often hard to get Hispanic parents to meetings at school. They may feel uncomfortable. Meeting them at their homes or at locations where they are more comfortable offers the best chance of getting them involved.

- Show affection. Be warm and friendly. Treat them the way they are likely to treat you—as family.

Be Welcoming and Foster Warm Relationships

Hispanic/Latino children usually are raised in the cocoon of their protective families. They are taught to be respectful and obedient. Their personalities reflect their culture—they tend to be more physically affectionate, warmer, and more concerned about others than their non-Hispanic/Latino counterparts. Touches, hugs, and handshakes are common. That is what they are used to; that is what they expect.

They are likely to feel uncomfortable in a new setting. These feelings are intensified if they do not speak English or do not speak it well. They need to feel safe. They want the teacher to care about them like their family does. They want to be friendly with the other children; they do not like to be made fun of because they come from a different culture and speak another language.

It is important to make sure no child is ostracized because he is from a different racial or ethnic group or is non-English speaking. All children need to feel proud of their culture and heritage.

Teachers need to create an environment where differences are respected and appreciated.

If children do not feel wanted and secure, learning and relationships will be difficult.

What to Do

- Invite family members to join boys on the first day of your program. Having someone from their family in the classroom initially will give boys a sense of security and ease the transition. It will also help the family understand what you are trying to accomplish.
- Welcome each child warmly into the classroom. Greet the child and his family member by name and with a Spanish-language greeting. Introduce him to the other children, who welcome him the same way. Show everyone how pleased you are to have him in the program. Identify another child to be a big or little "brother."
- Make sure someone in the classroom speaks Spanish. If the child and his family member do not speak English well, make sure an aide or someone else in the classroom can translate for them and for you.
- Tell the other children about his culture. Spend some time reading a book about the country he comes from—or plan a lunch with a popular dish that reflects his culture.
- Teach the children some words in Spanish. Choose something you are learning about, and teach the children a few related words. For example, if you are learning colors, teach the class the Spanish words for red (*rojo*), yellow (*amarillo*), and blue (*azul*).
- Show affection with hugs, handshakes, and pats on the back. More than most American boys, Hispanic/Latino boys are used to lots of physical signs of affection, including hugs. Pat them on the back or on the arm or give hugs or handshakes when they do something well.

Reflect and Celebrate Hispanic/Latino Culture

Family is the center of life for Hispanic/Latino boys. They may be fearful and uncomfortable in settings outside the home. This can cause stress that tends to occupy their minds and inhibit learning. Boys seem to have greater problems with this than girls. To help them settle in and feel secure, include items that represent the Hispanic/Latino culture—and the cultures of all the children—not just the usual visual aids, most of which are geared to the mainstream culture.

What to Do

- Create a familiar physical environment. For Hispanic/Latino boys to feel comfortable in the classroom, they need to see items that remind them of home and people who look like them and their families. Encourage them—and all the children—to bring in family photos and post them. Make sure visual learning aids, posters, and pictures include Hispanic/Latino people and include places they know.

- Give children opportunities to share information about their heritage, family, and traditions. Have children bring in items from home or foods or crafts that represent their heritage and family. Ask them to talk about special things their families or friends do on holidays or other special occasions. Often mothers, grandmothers, aunts, and other members of the family will happily bring in huge quantities of Mexican, Cuban, or Puerto Rican food to share for parties or other special occasions.

- Celebrate special days. Along with American holidays, celebrate National Hispanic Heritage Month (September 15 to October 15) and Hispanic/Latino holidays such as Cinco de Mayo (May 5), Día de Acción de Gracias (Hispanic Thanksgiving—same day as regular U.S. Thanksgiving), and regional festivals such as the Calle Ocho festival in Miami. (For more information, see http://www.hispanic-culture-online.com/hispanic-holidays.html#axzz2HPf2ebnX.) Ask the family what days are most important and how they celebrate them, and see if they want to participate in classroom festivities. This will enhance the family feeling. It will also teach the other children in the classroom about customs and traditions in a fun way and will increase their understanding and appreciation.

- Post pictures and posters of notable Hispanics and Latinos. Make sure the classroom has images of Hispanics and Latinos in different roles, including people such as Cesar Chavez, labor leader; Sonia Sotomayor, associate justice, U.S. Supreme Court; Severo Ochoa, winner of the Nobel Prize in Medicine; Ralph de la Vega, president and CEO of AT&T; U.S. Senator Bob Menendez (NJ); Franklin R. Chang-Díaz, astronaut; Carlos Eire, writer, winner of the 2003 National Book Award; Jaime Escalante, the teacher who inspired the film *Stand and Deliver*; and of course many ballplayers and entertainers. Featuring these people also gives you a chance to talk about different careers. (We suggest you feature only one ballplayer and one entertainer to put the focus on other occupations the boys may not be aware of.)

- Create opportunities for boys to learn about the work, family, and community experiences of successful local Hispanics/ Latinos. Bring fathers, male relatives of children, and exemplary males from the community into the classroom to talk about their lives and their work and to participate in classroom and outside activities.

- Read and discuss books about Hispanics/Latinos:
    - Try age-appropriate stories of high-achieving Hispanic/ Latino males that show how these people grew up and how they became successful.
    - Read stories about Hispanic/Latino children, their lives, and their problems and how they surmounted them.

- Make sure books on Hispanics/Latinos are visible in the classroom. You will find a librarian-recommended list in the Resources section of this book.

Set High Expectations

Setting high expectations is important to any boy who is disadvantaged by poverty, language, physical disability, or other difficulties. We covered this in the chapter on African American boys, and it bears repeating here. Low expectations equal poor performance. High expectations yield the highest results.

Setting Hispanic/Latino boys on a path to success in school is important. Their families may be warm and loving but may not know how to help them achieve in this new environment. If a boy is behind others because of his language difficulties, redouble your efforts to bring him up to speed. He has been taught to be obedient, and he will likely want to please you—so set your expectations high, and see how far he can go. When he succeeds, he will add the self-confidence he needs to be successful in the next test.

What to Do

■ Show them you love learning new things. Convey a love of learning with a positive attitude and creative ways to teach. Spur their interest by connecting learning to their heritage; teach them things they do not know about their own culture. Teach them about things that interest them, and encourage them to explore different activity areas on their own. Instill the value of education, and communicate that education is for everyone.

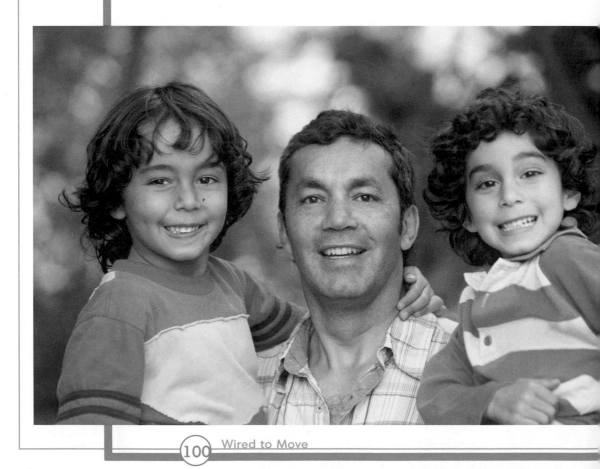

- Let them know you believe in their abilities. Hispanic/Latino boys can feel at a disadvantage because they do not speak English well or feel they are different in spite of your efforts to convince them otherwise. Give them lots of positive reinforcement. Your praise will mean a great deal.

- Learn about, discuss, and support their hopes and dreams. Start them thinking about what they could become when they grow up. What do they like to do? Discuss the importance of doing well in school, and talk about college. Let them know they can be whatever they choose if they work hard enough and get an education. Encourage them to follow their hopes and dreams.

- Expose them to different occupations. Introduce them to interesting occupations beyond what they are exposed to in their homes and families. Give them a sense of what these people accomplish—doctors healing people and coming up with cures for diseases, lawyers fighting for justice, firefighters saving people from disasters, and so on.

- Encourage them to take initiative and learn about and do new things. Give them opportunities to make choices and suggestions, explore things that interest them, and move beyond their comfort zones.

- Encourage them to think for themselves, not follow others. Read stories about and discuss challenges, issues, and obstacles boys face. Ask what they would do in similar circumstances. Let them think about and answer some of their own questions where appropriate. Give them opportunities to make choices.

- Set concrete goals. Help them set goals so they get in the habit. When boys have goals and achieve them, they gain confidence.

- Believe these boys can achieve excellence whatever their circumstances. Whether boys are slow learners, have behavior problems, or are top performers, always believe in them and work with them to be their best, building on their strengths and helping them overcome their limitations.

Create a Sense of Community

The family dynamic that is so strong in Hispanic/Latino families creates a sense of community in their children. They are taught to be cooperative, not in competition with, other members of their families and ethnic group. In young Hispanic/Latino boys, nurture trumps nature. They like to work together. They also tend to be more concerned about others than typical boys of their age.

Teachers are admired and respected. Boys see them the same way they perceive their mothers, who are the heart of the home. Hispanic/Latino boys are comfortable and are more likely to do their best in a classroom that mirrors the cooperative community they know and understand.

This is even more critical for children from migrant families who move from place to place in search of seasonal work and often team up with other families to share their scarce resources. Their stability is in each other, not in a home. A classroom that feels like home can be an oasis for them.

What to Do

- Foster a sense of classroom unity. Stress working together for the good of everyone in the classroom. Develop projects that involve all the children. Give praise and recognition when children accomplish things as a group. Refer to the classroom as *our*, not *the*, classroom.
- Let boys work in teams. Hispanic/Latino boys do well when they work together as part of a team. This is a comfortable way for them to learn.
- Emphasize group decision making and problem solving. Where appropriate, let children make choices and work out problems on issues that affect them as a whole.
- Do not discipline boys in front of other children. While this is a good strategy for all children, it is even more important for Hispanic/Latino boys for whom the group is especially strong. See the section on "Use Constructive Approaches to Discipline."

RESOURCES USED IN THIS CHAPTER

Galan, Fernando J. 1998. "An Empowerment Prevention Approach for Hispanic Youth." *The Prevention Researcher* 5(1): 10-12.

Jones, Toni Griego, and Mary Lou Fuller. 2003. *Teaching Hispanic Children*. Boston: Allyn & Bacon.

Lopez-Baez, Sandra. 1999. "Marianisimo." In Jeffrey Scott Mio, Joseph E. Trimble, Patricia Arredondo, Harold E. Cheatham, and David Sue, eds, *Key words in Multicultural Interventions: A Dictionary*. Westport, CT: Greenwood.

Marin, Gerardo, and H.C. Triandis. 1985. "Allocentrism as an Important Characteristic of the Behavior of Latin American and Hispanics." In Diaz-Guerrero, Rogelio, ed. *Cross-Cultural and National Studies in Social Psychology*. Amsterdam: Elsevier Science Publishers.

Muniz, Felix. 2009. Notes to the author, October 15 (Unpublished).

Santiago-Rivera, Azara L., Patricia Arredondo, Martiza Gallardo-Cooper. 2002. *Counseling Latinos and La familia: A Practical Guide.* Thousand Oaks, CA: Sage Publications.

Vasquez, James A. 1998. "Distinctive Traits of Hispanic Students." *The Prevention Researcher* 5(1): 1-4.

PARTNERING WITH PARENTS

Facts and Strategies for Early Childhood Teachers

Young boys perform best when teachers, parents, and other family members work together. Research shows that parent involvement is directly related to success in school. Children receive higher grades and test scores and have better attendance at school and better attitudes toward school when family members are involved.

Boys enter early learning programs with already-formed patterns, shaped by their home lives. They have developed routines, perceptions, and views—including attitudes about school and learning—from

> *The frequency of parent–teacher contact and involvement at the early childhood education site is... associated with preschool performance.*
> *–Harvard Family Research Project*

their family members. In the 2008 CNN documentary series *Black in America—Men,* Soledad O'Brien profiles successful African American men. Whether they are from impoverished or affluent backgrounds, all say their parents and other family members helped them set goals and achieve. Boys who heed these messages from their families get engaged in school when they are young and do well throughout their educational careers.

To understand the boys they will be teaching, teachers need to know and be responsive to the families' lifestyles, cultures, challenges, and goals for their children. In turn, parents and other family members need to be on the same wavelength as teachers regarding the boys' development. Young boys become confused, and lessons may not take hold, if they learn one thing in the classroom and something else at home. From their early years on, they need to hear a consistent message from teachers, parents, and the culture at large: Do well in school so you can achieve success in work and in life.

The Harvard Family Research Project points out the importance of parent involvement to low-income children by citing the Chicago Child-Parent Centers experience, where they found "the home-school relationship buffers the negative impacts of poverty on the academic and behavioral outcomes of poor children. For example, children of low-income parents who participated in Chicago Child-Parent Centers (CPC) were more prepared for kindergarten, were less likely to be referred to special education, and later had higher rates of eighth grade reading achievement and high school completion and lower rates of grade retention."[18]

Getting parents and other family members involved in their boys' early childhood programs is not always easy. They are busy—many are dual-income or single-parent families, and time is difficult to find. Chances are they want the best for their children but may not know why family member participation should be a priority. Early childhood teachers can help families understand the importance

18 Harvard Family Research Project. 2006. "Family Involvement in Early Childhood Education," accessed December 9, 2011. http://www.hfrp.org/content/download/1181/48685/file/earlychildhood.pdf

of working together and can find creative ways to get them involved and share strategies and materials, despite their often-heavy schedules.

Collaborative partnerships with parents or other caretakers are critical to advancing young boys' positive development and ensuring consistency in learning and in physical and social-emotional development at home and in the classroom. Nurturing young boys must be a shared responsibility.

Communicate Warmly and Often

Engaging family members and fostering their participation is especially important when you are implementing boy-friendly strategies. Nurturing young boys is based on warm, honest, and ongoing two-way communication, mutual respect for one another, and agreement on what is best for them.

A welcoming space and warm, helpful staff establish a positive tone for parent-teacher relationships and set the stage for family members and staff to work together on the boys' behalf. The opposite is also true. Your classroom environment conveys an image of your program, and parents and other caretakers are quick to pick up the cues. Do they feel welcome and comfortable? Is the space clean, safe, and inviting? Are the staff warm and helpful? Do the teachers listen to what they have to say? Does the teacher show interest in their boy? Does anyone speak their language?

Teachers need to make parents and guardians feel welcome and valued, not only by greeting them warmly when they drop off or pick up the boys, but by collaborating on goals, keeping them informed, asking their opinions, sharing knowledge, and encouraging them to get involved in a variety of activities. This is important for all children, not only boys.

Why is it important? The experts give us many good reasons. According to the National Association for the Education of Young Children (NAEYC), "families who receive frequent and positive messages from teachers tend to become more involved in their children's education than do parents who do not receive this kind of communication."[19] Frequent parent-teacher communication has also been linked to higher quality of care and more sensitive interactions between children and teachers.[20, 21]

Families are our partners in nurturing young boys. They need to know what we know, and we need to know what they know. We need to have mutual goals and messages. Positive ongoing communication makes that happen.

What to Do

- Make communication with parents and other family members a priority. Develop a plan for communicating effectively with families on an ongoing basis, including policies and methods. Train staff.
- Learn about the boy and his family. Get to know the family's values, traditions, strengths, education, employment, and income, or other challenges the family may be facing; learn the family's hopes and goals for the child, including perceptions of the boy's strengths, his limitations, and obstacles he may face in learning. Plan a home visit—especially important for at-risk boys and those who do not speak English.
- Make sure classrooms and staff are welcoming to family members. Classrooms should be clean, well organized, and inviting. Have family photos and boys' drawings of their families on display. Allow family members to visit classrooms at any time. Always greet parents and other caregivers warmly, with a smile, and show interest.
- Hold an orientation for family members of newly enrolled children. Go over program goals, policies, curriculum, and opportunities for parent and other caregiver participation. Have a question-and-answer session.

19 National Association for the Education of Young Children. "Building Parent-Teacher Relationships," accessed December 10, 2011. www.naeyc.org/families/PT
20 Ghazvini, Alisa S., and Christine A. Readdick. 1994. "Parent-Caregiver Communication and Quality of Care in Diverse Child Care Settings." *Early Childhood Research Quarterly* 9(2): 207–22.
21 Owen, Margaret T., Anne M. Ware, and Bill Barfoot. 2000. "Caregiver-Mother Partnership Behavior and the Quality of Caregiver-Child and Mother-Child Interactions." *Early Childhood Research Quarterly* 15(3): 413–28.

- Give positive feedback on children every day. Make sure you tell family members at least one positive thing about their boy every day. Share insights. If the boy has done something inappropriate, address this in a positive way wherever possible, such as "He needs to work on...."

- Have translators available. Make sure you have a staff member or volunteer who can speak the language of boys who either do not speak English or do not speak it well. Accommodate language and cultural differences.

- Hold parent/caregiver conferences. Schedule individual conferences at least twice a year to go over each boy's progress with his parents or caregiver; set goals and strategies. Offer child care. Create an environment where family members feel comfortable enough to share information and concerns, ask questions, and collaborate on goals and strategies for the boy. Ensure sufficient time for adequate discussion.

- Notify parents and other caregivers of important happenings in a timely manner. Make sure to have clear, understandable policies and procedures for notifying family members of activities, events, field trips, menus, staff changes, emergencies, program closings, holidays, and other events. Communicate these to families verbally and in writing (school calendars; notices in cubby, backpack, notice boards; websites, e-mail, phone/text) and in a timely fashion. Consider creating a simple newsletter.

- Accommodate family members' schedules. Make sure you schedule meetings and events after work, on Saturdays, or at other times that accommodate family members' work schedules.

- Have a suggestion box. Give parents and other caregivers the opportunity to anonymously drop suggestions in a box placed in a visible location. Carefully consider these suggestions. If a suggestion is adopted, communicate to families that it came from the suggestion box.

- Have a complaint procedure. Make sure you have a process where parents and other family members can present complaints. Communicate the process to the families verbally and in writing at the initial family information session. Regard complaints as constructive criticism and worthy of careful consideration.

- Conduct parent-satisfaction surveys. Survey family members throughout the school year to determine satisfaction levels regarding program, staff, physical facility, and so on. Carefully consider responses, and incorporate and communicate changes where necessary.

Encourage Family Participation

The more parents and other family members are involved in your early childhood program, the better your success will be in implementing boy-friendly strategies. You will be in regular contact with the families, communicating regularly about their sons and working together to help the boys do their best.

Encouraging parents and other caregivers to participate in your program in as many ways as possible is in everybody's interest. It gives families a greater understanding of your methods, your teaching style, the curriculum, developmentally appropriate practices, and the strategies that are so important for their sons' development. Understanding leads to commitment, and you can expect the classroom strategies to transfer much more readily to the home. You will also learn a lot more about the boys' families—their values, their strengths, and their challenges—and that can help you better understand and address each boy's individual needs.

Families can participate in many ways. But getting them started is not always easy. They are busy. Both parents may work, or only one parent may be available to handle the dual responsibilities of work and home. So chances are, you will want to think about offering incentives, at least at first, and work to accommodate their schedules.

What to Do

- Invite parents and other family members to visit classrooms. From the beginning, make it clear to them that they are not only welcome but encouraged to visit classrooms at any time.

This can help their boys feel more comfortable. Plus, they are likely to learn some things they can follow through with at home—and you will learn more about working with them.

- Invite parents and other family members to assist with school activities and functions. Whenever you go on a field trip or host an event, invite the family members to come and help out. Have them help prepare classroom materials, read to the children, or work on craft or construction projects. This will be helpful for you and fun for them and their boys.

- Make use of family members' special talents, abilities, and experiences. Perhaps someone in the family plays an instrument, is artistic, or has an interesting occupation, background, or experience. Or, perhaps someone would like to share a cultural tradition on a special day. Invite family members to share with the children in the classroom. Especially important is for boys to see their fathers or brothers in the classroom.

- Establish a parent advisory committee. Give parents and other family members a role in making program decisions relating to their boys' care and education, family activities, and family learning opportunities. The more involved families are, the more they will understand the teacher's goals for their boys. Though you want family members involved in decisions, make sure you maintain the responsibility for ensuring developmentally appropriate practices in the classroom.

- Welcome family members and volunteers. Identify areas where you can use volunteers. Develop clear job descriptions. Post and distribute a list of opportunities to families with a note that encourages them to volunteer.

- Host family-oriented events. Hold occasional parent/child/teacher/staff events where families can gather in a social setting to meet and get to know one another, enjoy good food, and share experiences and ideas. Involve families in planning, organizing, bringing food, decorating, sharing cultural traditions, and so on. For example, hold potluck dinners, holiday and Mother's and Father's Day celebrations, and multicultural events.

Share Boy-Friendly Strategies

It is important that teachers and families be consistent in what they are teaching young boys. Collaborative partnerships with parents and other family members are critical to advancing a boy's positive development and ensuring consistency at home and in the classroom. The more you work together to further a boy's learning and social/emotional skills, the more likely he is to be successful. The more families know about working with boys, the better your boy-friendly classroom strategies will work.

Parents and other caregivers come from many different income levels and educational and cultural backgrounds. They have their own occupations and parenting styles. They are not likely to be aware of many of the boy-friendly strategies we have discussed in this book, or other important aspects of children's learning. Or, they may be in difficult situations and need help themselves. All of these things affect the boys you are teaching. If you do not address them, the boys and your teaching may suffer.

In many ways, your early childhood program can assist parents and other family members by sharing knowledge and by making them aware of resources in the community.

What to Do
- Have a monthly family night to help parents and other family members gain knowledge and understanding of children's educational and developmental needs and activities. Identify family members' needs and interests and a theme for each session. Be sure to include sessions on boys' brain tendencies

and boy-friendly strategies, allowing time for questions and answers. Encourage family members and teaching staff to share concerns and develop strategies to address them in school and at home.

- Host periodic family workshops. Bring in outside experts or collaborate with other early childhood programs to conduct in-depth workshops on why boys act the way they do (boy-friendly facts and strategies) and other topics important for families of boys, such as what media children should watch, choosing the right toys, or working with an early childhood teacher. Consider workshops on parenting skills, nutrition, behavior management, safety and health, recognition of child abuse, sudden infant death syndrome, healthy eating, emergency first aid, and so on, as determined by your parent advisory committee or parent surveys.

- Offer child care and other incentives for family members to come to family nights and family workshops. Having food is always a good bet, especially for working parents and other guardians who might enjoy not having to cook after a long day's work. Be sure to accommodate their schedules as much as possible.

- Offer reading materials. Establish a lending library and distribute family-education materials. Let parents and other caregivers borrow books of interest to boys and books, magazines, and videos on important early childhood topics for themselves. Make copies of interesting articles, materials from the NAEYC, and so on, and include them in children's folders. You will find flyers on boy-friendly and media strategies you can reproduce for parents and other caregivers in the Handouts for Parents and Other Caregivers section of this book.

- Show parents and other family members how they can supplement classroom learning at home. Give them information on things they can do to encourage learning and ensure consistency with what the boys are learning at school. Discuss with the families, get their feedback, and give them a handout like the one in the Handouts for Parents and Other Caregivers section of this book.

- Alert parents and other caregivers to community events and educational offerings for young children and their families. Promote constructive activities for young children by posting and distributing information on appropriate family/child events in the community. Encourage families to get involved in advocacy activities for children.
- Develop a community resource center or website link for parents and others who may need assistance with family or children's problems. Include information on local parenting, educational, and social service organizations. Include lists of community resources with enrollment/orientation packets. You may be able to get one from a community organization such as the United Way.

PARENT NIGHTS REINFORCE STRATEGIES FOR WORKING WITH BOYS

Our pilot Boys' Project centers hold parent nights once a month, at the after-work times agreeable to the most parents and other caregivers. There is always good food, good conversation, sharing ideas, and a speaker on an important early childhood topic. Lately we have spent a lot of time covering boys' issues—bringing in speakers to give families ideas on how to manage boys at home. We also give them handout cards with quick tips on working with boys. The family members are enthusiastic about these events; so are the teachers.

Empower Single Mothers

Single mothers should be praised for having the strength to raise children on their own. It is double the work—and it can be lonely and exhausting. Many of these mothers are struggling to make ends meet, further their education, or work full-time jobs while raising their children. They are stressed and find it hard to do all the things they want to do for their children.

They often feel their sons need guidance from a male; they are not sure how to handle them. These mothers, in particular, benefit from discussing their boys with teachers and from mentoring programs that bring fatherless boys together with adult males. Do your best to empower them and show them they can be successful in raising their boys.

What to Do

- Give them confidence they can be successful mothers to boys. Give them positive reinforcement. Praise their and their boys' accomplishments. Point to the examples of successful men who have been raised by single mothers. Examples include President Barack Obama, former President Bill Clinton, Dr. Ben Carson, Bill Cosby, Alexander Haig Jr., and Michael Phelps. Recommend books and films about successful single mothers—for example, *Gifted Hands: The Ben Carson Story*.
- Pass on helpful information. Even more than other family members, single mothers need good information on parenting, boys' learning, and how to help their sons grow and thrive. Share information wherever possible and recommend videos, books, and other resources.
- Recommend mentoring programs such as Big Brothers Big Sisters. Critical for boys is that they have positive male role models in their lives. If they do not have them, they will find their own—and their role models might be the neighborhood guy who drives the fancy car and sells drugs for a living. If no father or responsible male is available in a boy's life, some programs provide male volunteers who take boys on outings and provide a constructive influence. You will find a list in the Resources section of this book.

Have a Father-Friendly Program

We have talked about the importance of male role models for boys. No more important role models exist for boys than their fathers. Fathers play unique roles in their sons' development. Fathers are more likely than mothers to

- promote their children's intellectual and social development through physical play, which boys need to jog their brains;
- emphasize independence and allow boys more freedom to explore their surroundings, take risks, and challenge themselves; and
- push their sons to higher levels of achievement.

In their 1999 study, "Effects of Father Participation in Child Rearing: Twenty-Year Follow-Up," Edith Williams and Norma Radin found that fathers involved in their child's early care have a "significant influence, particularly on sons" who "learn by observing their fathers and modeling their problem-solving strategies, vocabulary and other behavior." The study concludes that active participation by fathers in rearing their children may be necessary.

That applies to involving fathers in early learning programs. Unfortunately, it is often hard to get fathers to participate. Mothers are usually the gatekeepers who handle these duties. Fathers may be reluctant and feel unwelcome. Staff may not reach out to them, often because they do not understand the importance of fathers' participation. Or, their programs may not be designed to involve fathers.

That needs to change, especially for the boys in the classroom.

What to Do

- Create a father-friendly environment. Greet every father warmly when he comes into the classroom. Make sure he knows he is welcome in the classroom at any time. Tell him about any upcoming events for fathers and family members and other opportunities to participate or help out. Show him examples of his child's work. Tell him at least one good thing his child did that day or the previous day.
- Communicate to both parents. Make sure to include the father in all correspondence, e-mails, and forms, even if he lives in a separate residence from the child. Have lines on forms for both parents to sign. (Many of the strategies mentioned in this section apply to mothers as well. They are repeated here to stress the importance of singling out and welcoming often-reluctant fathers.)
- Present expectations of fathers' participation at children's enrollment. In initial meetings prior to their child's enrollment, try to meet with both parents and explain the importance that both participate. Outline possibilities for participation, and try to get a commitment.
- Survey fathers on participation preferences. At the time of enrollment or, if this is not convenient, at another meeting with parents, give them separate surveys to complete asking about the kinds of participation they would like to see, their available days and hours, and so on. Having mothers

and fathers fill these out separately will allow you to create activities specifically for the fathers.

- Display pictures of fathers with their children in the classroom. You will want to showcase photos of the children's entire families—but make sure some photos show fathers interacting with their children and especially their sons in a variety of ways.

- Train staff on the importance of father participation and ways to create father-friendly classrooms. All staff need to be aware of the priority of making classrooms father friendly. Train them in what they can do to make their classrooms more welcoming to fathers.

- Create casual, family-oriented, and father/child-only activities. Depending on the participation preferences stated by the fathers in the survey, develop a schedule of activities aimed at involving them with their child's learning, educating them on parenting young children, or just having fun in family-oriented or father/child activities.

- Have at least one special father/son or father/child activity each school year. Single out fathers for at least one special event a year with their sons or children who attend your program.

- Invite fathers to participate in the classroom, on committees, and as volunteers. Invite fathers to come in and read to the children or to talk about their occupations or special hobbies. Ask them to serve on committees (make sure to have at least two male committee members so they will not feel overwhelmed). If a father has a special ability or talent that can aid the center, or if he just wants to help out, see if he will be a volunteer.

- Accommodate fathers' work schedules. Schedule activities after work hours or on weekends, using information from the survey.

- Make father-friendly resource lists available. Have a list available of resources for fathers: mentoring programs, constructive activities they can do with their sons, and organizations that can help with a variety of issues. Keep these readily available for them to pick up when they are in the center.

- Show appreciation for participation in unique ways. Have children make cards or pictures as gifts, showing things they like to do with their fathers. Send notes to fathers after they have participated in a program or activity at the center. Many fathers need a little extra push to get involved. Giving them special attention is one way to remove the barriers.

MAKING FATHERS FEEL WELCOME

When fathers come into early learning centers here, the first thing they are likely to see is a huge poster that tells them this is a father-friendly center.

That is just the beginning. Welcoming staff know how important fathers are to the children, especially to the boys, and go out of their way to let them know they are valued. Fathers are expected to be as involved as mothers and are given opportunities to serve as volunteers and on committees.

To help our Universal Prekindergarten (UPK) sites become more father-friendly, Starting Point created a manual on

HERE,
FATHER$ COUNT

We Have a Father-Friendly Program.
That Means We Value Your Input and Participation in the Care and Education of Your Children.

For More Information and Links to Resources, Services and Opportunities for Fathers, Contact Starting Point at 216-575-0061 or online at www.starting-point.org

4600 Euclid Avenue, Suite 500, Cleveland, OH 44103

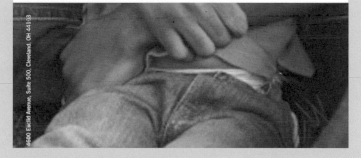

creating father-friendly programs. Each of the sites is asked to host an event just for fathers and their children; for example, Donuts with Dudes; Read to Me, Daddy; and Bring Your Dad to School Day. The Cleveland Children's Museum is involved, too. The museum has held Dad's Night Out events (each one attended by more than one hundred people) and has brought its Crafty Chemistry Project to 11 different sites, giving dads, other male family members, and the children an opportunity to learn about chemistry and make "slime."

RESOURCES USED IN THIS CHAPTER

Harvard Family Research Project. 2006. "Family Involvement in Early Childhood Education," accessed December 9, 2011. http://www.hfrp.org/content/downlaod/1181/48685/file/earlychildhood.pdf.

National Association for the Education of Young Children. "Engaging Diverse Families," accessed December 10, 2011. www.naeyc.org/families/PT

Ou, Suh-Ruu. 2005. "Pathways of Long-term Intervention Program on Educational Attainment: Findings from the Chicago Longitudinal Study." *Applied Developmental Psychology*. 26(5), 578–611.

Williams, Edith, and Norma Radin. 1999. "Effects of Father Participation in Child Rearing: Twenty-Year Follow-Up." *American Journal of Orthopsychiatry*. 69(3): 328-36.

LIMITING MEDIA INFLUENCES

The explosion of media influences—children's television shows, DVDs, video games, and computers—is such a recent phenomenon that we have had little scientific data on its effects on young children until recently. Now the evidence is beginning to trickle in. Studies are backing up what many educators have long believed—that young children are spending far too much time in front of screens. This is upsetting everything from language development to healthy nutrition and motor-skill development.

Many early childhood teachers respond, "Our students do not watch TV or play video games. We give them constructive play and learning opportunities."

> *The mass media have come to rival parents, school and religion as the most influential institution in children's lives.*
> —Media & Values

And they are mostly right. Early childhood teachers do encourage active, constructive activities. But a study conducted by the Center for Child Health, Behavior, and Development at Seattle Children's Research Institute found that

- preschool children in home-based child care watch TV for 2.4 hours per day on average, and
- preschool children in center-based settings average 24 minutes of TV time per day.[22]

Add that to the average preschooler's two to three daily hours of TV time at home, and you have four to five-and-a-half hours of total daily TV viewing for children who attend family child care programs and two-and-a-half to three-and-a-half hours for children in center programs.

That is not all. Children as young as three are also spending time watching DVDs, playing video games, and using computers. That adds more hours of screen time for children, a disturbing trend and far more than the experts recommend. Here is what they say:

The American Academy of Pediatrics (AAP) recommends that children three to six years old be limited to no more than two hours of screen time of all types per day. Children two and under should not watch TV at all.

In addition, NAEYC and the Fred Rogers Center issued the following recommendations on technology use for early childhood educators:

1. Select, use, integrate, and evaluate technology and interactive media tools in intentional and developmentally appropriate ways, giving careful attention to the appropriateness and quality of the content, the child's experience, and the opportunities for co-engagement.
2. Provide a balance of activities in programs for young children, recognizing that technology and interactive media can be valuable tools when used intentionally with children to

---

22 Christakis, Dimitri, and Michelle Garrison. 2009. "Preschool-Aged Children's Television Viewing in Child Care Settings." Pediatrics 124(6): 1627–1632.

extend and support active, hands-on, creative, and authentic engagement with those around them and with their world.

3. Prohibit the passive use of television, videos, DVDs, and other noninteractive technologies and media in early childhood programs for children younger than two, and discourage passive and noninteractive uses with children ages two through five.

4. Limit any use of technology and interactive media in programs for children younger than two to those that appropriately support responsive interactions between caregivers and children and that strengthen adult-child relationships.

5. Carefully consider the screen-time recommendations from public health organizations for children from birth through age five when determining appropriate limits on technology and media use in early childhood settings. Screen time estimates should include time spent in front of a screen at the early childhood program and, with input from parents and families, at home and elsewhere.[23]

Provide leadership in ensuring equitable access to technology and interactive media experiences for the children in their care and for parents and families.

TV, Video, and DVD Use among Young Children

A study by Elizabeth Vandewater and her team at the University of Texas found that children spend more time watching TV than on any other single free-time activity. Nearly 40 percent of families with children from birth to age four say they have television sets turned on most of the time. (Please see Table 6.1, Media Access and Use by Children Zero to Six.) The percentage is even higher among single parents. These children spend less time playing creatively and interacting with their families. Even

---

23 National Association for the Education of Young Children and the Fred Rogers Center for Early Learning and Children's Media at Saint Vincent College. 2012. *Technologly and Interactiue Media as Tools in Early Childhood Programs Serving Children from Birth through Age 8.* Washington, DC: NAEYC.

when the television is just on in the background and no one is actively watching, children are distracted, and playtime suffers.

The same study also indicated that around one-third of children from three to six have working televisions in their bedrooms. This is troubling. According to the AAP, bedroom television has been linked to poor academic, social, and physical activity outcomes. Parents gave various reasons why they did this: "other family members wanted to watch other programs"; "it helps put them to sleep"; "it keeps them occupied so we can do other things"; and "it is a reward for good behavior." Another study by the Kaiser Family Foundation found that 53 percent of children eat at least one meal while watching TV.

Table 6.1
MEDIA ACCESS AND USE BY CHILDREN ZERO TO SIX
■ Of children zero to two, 90 percent watch some television every day.
■ One-third of three- to six-year-olds have a television in their bedroom.
■ Of children zero to six, 75 percent watch television and 32 percent watch DVDs or videos each day.
■ Of five- to six-year-olds, 27 percent use a computer every day.
■ Thirteen percent of children ages three to four and 16 percent of children ages five to six play video games each day.
Elizabeth Vandewater et al. 2007. "Digital Childhood: Electronic Media and Technology Use among Infants, Toddlers, and Preschoolers." *Pediatrics* 119(5): 1005-1015.

The Effects of Screen Time on Young Children

Studies show that babies and toddlers learn best when they interact with family members, teachers, and other significant people in their lives—not from TV, videos, or DVDs. Bonding with an adult facilitates learning, especially for children two and under. For these children, watching DVDs that claim to create baby geniuses may actually end up delaying speech.

The younger children are, the more they need human interaction to learn. This is important for preschoolers, too. Children learn better from real people than from screen images.

TV also cuts into creative playtime, which is essential for children's intellectual and social development. As David Elkind notes in his 2008 book, *The Hurried Child*, "when playtime is withheld, brain growth is delayed."

Children need to touch things, move them around, and figure out how they work. They need to use their hands and exercise their brains. They need to find out how tall they can build a block tower before it falls and see how big their friends' eyes get when they look through a magnifier. This is how children learn to think, reason, and solve problems; develop fine and gross motor skills; and discover how to entertain themselves.

Children need bonding, brain stimulation, physical movement, and socialization. In her book, *Endangered Minds: Why Children Don't Think and What We Can Do About It*, psychologist Jane Healy tells us that television "suppresses mental activity by putting viewers in a trance." If true, this is especially troublesome for boys, whose brains tune out more readily than the brains of girls. As we have discussed, boys need movement to engage their brains.

Too much TV can also intensify attention problems, which are more prevalent in boys than girls. A 2004 study of one- and three-year-olds by the Child Health Institute of the University of Washington linked early television exposure to shorter attention spans by the time these children reached age seven. For each hour of television viewing, the risk increased 10 percent.

More recently, the journal *Pediatrics* published a study that looked at the immediate results of the effect of a fast-paced cartoon show (identified as *SpongeBob SquarePants*) on attention span, focus, and delayed gratification in a group of four-year-olds. The children who watched the show performed much more poorly on the tasks than children who watched an educational television show (PBS's *Caillou*) or drew with crayons or markers. The conclusion was that watching fast-paced programs like *SpongeBob* potentially has a negative effect on children's learning—showing that the nature of the programming young children watch is an important factor. An NAEYC article suggests that, in addition to this study's implications for television watching, early education teachers might consider alternating periods of high activity with projects that require intense focus.

TV watching has also been linked to the increasing rates of obesity among children. In July 2011, the AAP cited studies in the United States, the United Kingdom, New Zealand, and Japan that clearly show the correlation between TV and obesity in age groups from 3 to 30. According to the academy, TV watching leads to a more sedentary lifestyle, which limits physical activity, contributes to unhealthy eating practices learned from TV programs and advertising, increases snacking, and interferes with normal sleep patterns—all related to obesity. (Please see Table 6.2.)

The academy also referenced another study that linked bedroom TVs to obesity. It stated that a full 40 percent of the obese one- to four-year-old children in the study had TVs in their bedrooms, which increased TV watching and sedentary activity.

When young children are watching TV, it is best to limit the time and have a parent watching with them to help them understand what they are seeing and answer their questions.

When family members tune into a program for themselves or have it on in the background, even when no one is actively watching, this distracts both the family member and the child—decreasing interaction and interfering with play and activities.

Not all TV is bad, but some of the most popular children's TV programs offer poor examples of how people speak and relate to one another. Two- to four-year-olds learn from what they see others do, and that includes the TV characters they watch on television. If the characters are punching or hitting or talking disrespectfully, the children may follow their example. Programs with advertising aimed at children may create demands for products that are far from beneficial.

EFFECTS OF THE MEDIA

- *Media violence can lead to aggressive behavior in children. It especially damages young children because they cannot easily tell the difference between real life and fantasy.*
- *Violence in Saturday-morning cartoons is higher than during prime time.*
- *Before the age of 18, the average child will witness more than 200,000 acts of violence on television, including 16,000 murders.*
- *Longitudinal studies found that 8-year-old boys who viewed the most violent programs while growing up were more likely to participate in aggressive and delinquent behavior by age 18.*
- *The average African American household watches 77.3 hours of TV per week, compared to 50.1 hours per week for all other American households.*
- *By age 16, the average American will witness 25,000 sexual acts outside of marriage on TV.*
- *On average, American adolescents listen to music and watch music videos 40 hours a week—more time than they spend with their friends outside of school or watching TV.*
- *Children of all ages use music to gather information about the adult world, withdraw from social contact, facilitate friendships, and help create a personal identity.*
- *Music alters and intensifies moods, furnishes slang, dominates conversations, and provides ambiance at their gatherings.*
- *Music personalities provide models for how they act and dress.*

American Academy of Pediatrics. 2009. "Media Violence" *Pediatrics* 124(5): 1495-1503.
American Academy of Pediatrics. 2009. "Impact of Music, Music Lyrics and Music Videos on Children and Youth" *Pediatrics* 124(5): 1488-1494.
Rigby, Jill. 2006. *Respectful Children in a Disrespectful World.* New York: Howard Books.

What about Educational TV, Videos, and DVDs?

As we have said, real people and real play are most important to a child's growth and development. For children age two and younger, there is no evidence that television, even educational television, has any benefit.

Children older than age two can learn from the right kinds of educational television shows and videos or DVDs. Choosing programs with simple story lines that expose children to new things and new worlds or feature simple messages such as being nice to others and saying *please* and *thank you* is important. In her book *Into the Minds of Babes: How Screen Time Affects Children from Birth to Age Five*, Lisa Guernsey says young children need to absorb what they are hearing and seeing. They get confused if a story changes time or place without a logical transition or cuts too quickly from one scene to another. If a child is trying to figure out what is happening on screen, the lessons are lost.

One of the shows that meets the criteria is *Sesame Street*, which conducts extensive testing and makes programming changes as a result of its findings. Others are *Barney, Blue's Clues, Dragon Tales,* and *Dora the Explorer*. Programs with some interaction, such as *Blue's Clues*, are especially effective for young viewers. In studies of these programs, *Blue's Clues* scored well in flexible thinking among three- to five-year-olds; *Barney* did well on vocabulary, manners, and health education. Interestingly, the scores were even higher when a teacher was present to give additional instruction. Other children's shows such as *The Wiggles* encourage needed physical activity.

Note that, importantly, many children's TV shows

do not test their effects
on their young audiences.
And they should. Some have educational consultants, but that
alone does not mean these shows are instructive.

Research has demonstrated that preschool children can gain
academically and socially from the right kind of educational
programming. For children living in disadvantaged households
where adults rarely talk to their children, educational programs
can be helpful. A cooperative initiative between the U.S.
Department of Education and the Ready to Learn program of
PBS Kids and the Corporation for Public Broadcasting aims to
harness the potential of public television to aid children living in
poverty, with literacy and math programming, materials, teacher
guides, and much more. Literacy programs such as *Martha
Speaks*, *Super Why*, and *WordWorld* have been developed, others
are planned, and pilot programs in PBS markets are testing the
effectiveness of the new content.

The same rules apply to videos and websites. Guernsey says
some videos stimulate imaginative play and good behavior, and
websites with games such as *Peep and the Big Wide World* and
Curious George employ a scaffolding approach where children
can progress from one step to another at their own speed. But,
again, the length of screen time still needs to be limited.

Table 6.2
AMERICAN ACADEMY OF PEDIATRICS (AAP)
2011 Media Use Recommendations

- The AAP discourages TV and media use by children younger than two years.

- The AAP recommends no more than two hours of screen time for children three to six.

- The AAP realizes that media exposure is a reality for many families in today's society. If parents and other caregivers choose to engage their young children with electronic media, they should have concrete strategies to manage it. Ideally, caregivers should review the content of what their child is watching and watch the program with their child.

- Families are discouraged from placing a television set in their child's bedroom.

- Family members need to realize that their own media use can have a negative effect on their children. Television that is intended for adults and is on with a young child in the room is distracting for both the adult and the child.

- Unstructured playtime is more valuable for the developing brain than any electronic media exposure. If a parent is not able to actively play with a child, that child should have solo playtime with an adult nearby. Even for infants as young as four months, solo play allows a child to think creatively, problem solve, and accomplish tasks with minimal adult interaction. Family members can also learn something in the process of giving children an opportunity to entertain themselves while remaining nearby.

American Academy of Pediatrics Council on Communications and Media. 2011. "Media use by Children Younger Than 2 Years." *Pediatrics* 128(5): 1040–1045. http://pediatrics.aappublications. org/content/128/5/1040.full.pdf+html.

Jordan, Amy, James Hersey, Judith McDivitt, and Carrie Heitzler. 2006. "Reducing Children's Television Viewing Time: A Qualitative Study of Parents and Their Children." *Pediatrics* 18(5): e1301-e1310.

What about Video and Computer Games?

Video games are everywhere today. Even preschoolers have them. Some actually bring handheld video games to their early learning centers, much to the dismay of their teachers. Instead of seeing what they can build with LEGO bricks, many little boys' eyes are glued to their gaming devices.

Some parents look on electronic games as pacifiers or behavior-control tools for their children. Children are also influenced by their peers and by marketing campaigns. Consequently, young children are spending an average of seven hours a week on gaming–in addition to their other screen time. As families and teachers are finding out, it can be difficult to pry children away. Power struggles and tantrums are difficult enough to handle at this age. These devices add to the problem. They turn on the reward systems in children's brains.

Daniel Amen tells us that playing video games activates children's brains to release dopamine—a chemical triggered when something pleasurable happens. The more a child plays the game, the more stimulated his brain becomes and the more dopamine is released. When this happens, the parts of the cerebral cortex that control judgment and decision making shut down. Over time, many experts believe, this makes gaming addictive.

In their book *Video Games and Your Kids*, Hilarie Cash and Kim McDaniel say boys are especially vulnerable. They get caught up in the competitive, aggressive, and often violent nature of the games. For boys who are lonely; have low self-esteem or attention deficits; or suffer from abuse, neglect, autism, depression, or anxiety, video games fill the gaps and offer an escape.

Cash and McDaniel say game play uses only a small portion of the brain, which means other parts are not being stimulated. This impairs brain development. "If lopsided development occurs in the brains," they note, "the following problems are likely to occur":

■ Shortened attention span
■ Reduced critical thinking
■ Reduced creativity and imagination
■ Reduced ability to be internally motivated and self-directed
■ Lowered frustration tolerance
■ Cognitive desensitization (aggression)
■ Limited language development
■ Visual deficits (depth perception, nearsightedness, computer-vision syndrome)

Gaming works against developing verbal, physical, social, and decision-making skills and impulse control. Boys' reward centers demand more and more pleasure from gaming, meaning they have less and less interest in the constructive activities that build their brains and skills. Until age two, brain synapses form at the rate of 1.8 million per second; after that, unused synapses are discarded. How children use their developing brains is important.

Cash and McDaniel strongly recommend that parents not give children electronic gaming devices before age seven or eight, and that they should be off-limits to preschool children. As we have discussed, children from three to six need to explore, play, and discover the world around them. They are developing verbal, social, and physical skills. And they are learning about limits—how to control their impulses and make good choices.

Computer software for young children is often better than games created for gaming devices. Some feature animals or popular educational TV characters. But even here, families need to be vigilant and make good choices. The AAP recommends that children younger than five years old only play on-screen games that are developmentally appropriate and with an adult present to provide guidance.

TV and Video Game Violence

Common sense tells us we should keep young children away from violence, whether on TV, on television, on DVDs, in films, or in video games. Many caregivers still lug young children to movie theaters so they can see the latest action flicks—or have their main TV set tuned into the latest legal thrillers or murder stories. They assume it will not hurt the children. Research tells a different story.

As early as 12 months, young children pick up on-screen emotions and become scared when they see frightening scenes. Until age four, children do not really understand whether what they are seeing is real or a fantasy.

Four-year-olds understand the difference, but younger children do not, according to psychologists Adrienne Samuels and Marjorie Taylor, who have studied the concept. They have gauged children's reactions to frightening storybook illustrations and found that three-year-olds were confused about whether what they were seeing was real or not. Scary images for them produced considerable anxiety. Their studies offer a solid rationale for keeping young children away from violent or frightening material.

TV Ratings, V-Chips, and Parental Controls

Caregivers may choose among several ways to exercise some control over the television programming children watch. Most TV shows are rated according to age appropriateness and whether or not a program contains violence, sex, adult language, or suggestive dialogue. The ratings are as follows:

- TVY—All children, specifically designed for children ages two to six
- TVY7—Children seven and older
- TVG—General audience
- TVPG—Parental guidance suggested
- TV14—Unsuitable for children under 14; parents strongly cautioned
- TVMA—Mature audience only

These ratings may also contain letters indicating high levels of unsuitable material:

- D—Suggestive dialogue
- L—Coarse or crude language
- S—Sexual situations
- V—Violence
- FV—Fantasy violence (in children's programming)

These ratings can be found in the upper left-hand corner of the TV screen during the first 15 seconds of the program as well as in newspaper listings and cable TV guides. The programs are rated by episode, and the same show can have different ratings from day to day or week to week, depending on the episode's content. More information can be found at www.tvguidelines.org/ratings.htm.

It is also possible to block programs that are inappropriate for children, by using the V-chip and parental controls. Instructions are available in the television on-screen menu, in your owner's manual, via cable or satellite instructions, or by logging on to www.tvguidelines.org/parentalcontrols.htm.

Many video game systems, including Wii and Nintendo DSi, also have parental controls.

Facts and Strategies for Early Childhood Teachers

Whether or not you use media in your classroom—and studies indicate that many family child care homes and early learning centers do—you want to make sure the children in your care get the best possible start. As we have seen, TV, videos, DVDs, and video games can interfere with a child's development, so we hope you will use and pass this information on to your teachers and, most important, to the families of the children in your classrooms. Use your influence with the children as well. If you do have media in your classroom, make sure you choose programs well, offer added instruction, and keep the time to a minimum.

Children are inclined to learn from television [because] it is never too busy to talk to them, and it never has to brush them aside while it does household chores.
—National Commission of Causes and Prevention of Violence

Communicate Good Media Strategies to Families

Media—all types—exerts tremendous influence on boys. Too much or the wrong kinds of media can stifle brain development, creativity, exploration, and the physical activity so critical to boys' learning in the early years. Evidence also shows that too much screen time can lead to attention deficit problems, obesity, and other problems.

Home is where boys spend the bulk of their time on TV, videos, DVDs, and video games. It is important that teachers convey information to parents and other family members who may not be aware of the effects of these media on young boys and on children in general. This affects what teachers are trying to accomplish in the classroom.

What to Do

- Host a media education night. Discuss media strategies with family members and answer their questions. Bring in an expert on media effects on children and age-appropriate activities. Give a "Making Good Media Choices" sheet (found in the Handouts for Parents and Other Caregivers section of this book) to attendees.
- Collaborate with children's hospitals, pediatricians, and other early childhood centers to host community events or publicity programs to alert parents to the right media strategies.
- Send "Making Good Media Choices" flyers home with children. Ask the children to hand a flyer to their family members and tell them the teacher says it is important.
- Attach a magnetic strip to "Making Good Media Choices" so parents can place it on refrigerators.
- In child conferences or in talking with parents or other caregivers, stress the importance of managing media. Make sure family members understand why and how TV, videos, DVDs, the Internet, and video games can be harmful to children's learning. Encourage parents to limit media time and substitute outdoor play, reading, block building, and other active pursuits. Give them a copy of the "Making Good Media Choices" flyer.
- No video games. Post a "No Video Games Permitted" sign, and make sure family members understand that no video game devices are allowed in the early learning facility.
- Post "Making Good Media Choices" in an area of the classroom family members are likely to notice.

Use Recommended Media Strategies in the Classroom

Chances are most early learning facilities follow good practices and do not use media in their classrooms, unless it is limited and appropriate educational fare. Still, research shows that some centers and many family child care homes do use media, adding to the total hours a young child sits in front of the television set at home. All teachers need to be aware of the effects of too much or the wrong kinds of media on children. They need to follow good media strategies in the classroom and convey them to the children and their families.

The proliferation of media and technology and intense marketing makes it critical to understand, use, and pass this information on. Early childhood is the time when brain development takes place. Bonding with families and caregivers and playtime are the most important elements in children's development. Too much or the wrong kinds of media, however harmless they may seem, can impair learning ability and have other consequences. While this affects all children, boys are particularly vulnerable.

This may be one of today's most important issues, and early childhood teachers are in a position to have an effect.

What to Do

- Train teachers in appropriate media strategies for young children. Make sure all the teachers in your classrooms have a solid grounding in the effects of excessive media on young children and know the recommended media strategies.
- Use appropriate media strategies in all classrooms or family child care homes. That means no TV, videos, or DVDs unless they serve a sound educational purpose, are limited in time, and are accompanied by teacher instruction.
- Set rules for media use in classrooms, and convey them clearly to the children. Have rules governing media use, such as no video games or gaming devices are allowed, and make sure the children (and their family members) understand.
- Guide children on making good media choices. Talk about TV and video games and compare to play activities. Help children understand that doing is better than watching. Ask them questions about what they like to watch and do and why, and compare.
- Make media use a priority in communications with family members. Convey media information to families through posters, handouts, and presentations, and convey the importance of good media strategies.

RESOURCES USED IN THIS CHAPTER

American Academy of Pediatrics Council on Communications and Media. 2011. "Media Use by Children Younger Than 2 Years." *Pediatrics* 128(5): 1040–1045. http://pediatrics.aappublications.org/content/128/5/1040.full.pdf+html.

Cash, Hilarie, and Kim McDaniel. 2008. *Video Games and Your Kids: How Parents Stay in Control.* Enumclaw, WA: Issues Press.

Clay, Rebecca. 2003. "Unraveling New Media's Effects on Children." *American Psychological Association* 34(2): 40, accessed December 10, 2011. http://www.apa.org/monitor/feb03/unraveling.aspx.

Guernsey, Lisa. 2007. *Into the Minds of Babes: How Screen Time Affects Children from Birth to Age Five.* Philadelphia: Basic Books.

Healy, Jane M. 2004. "Early Television Exposure and Subsequent Attention Problems in Children." *Pediatrics* 113(4): 917–918.

Healy, Jane M. 1990. *Endangered Minds: Why Our Children Don't Think and What We Can Do about It.* New York: Simon & Schuster.

Jordan, Amy, James Hersey, Judith McDivitt, and Carrie Heitzler. 2006. "Reducing Children's Television Viewing Time: A Qualitative Study of Parents and Their Children." *Pediatrics* 118(5): e1303–e1310.

PBS. "Children and Media; TV & Movies: Preschoolers." PBS Parents, accessed December 15, 2011. http://www.pbs.org/parents/childrenandmedia/tvmovies-preschool.html.

Samuels, Adrienne and Marjorie Taylor. 1994. "Children's Ability to Distinguish Fantasy Events from Real-Life Events." *British Journal of Developmental Psychology* 12(4): 417–427.

Stelter, Brian. 2008. "Report Ties Children's Use of Media to Their Health." *New York Times*, December 1, accessed December 11, 2011. http://www.nytimes.com/2008/12/02/arts/02stud.html.

HEROES AND SUPERHEROES

Facts and Strategies for Early Childhood Teachers

Each person must live their life as a model for others.
—Rosa Parks

Boys need heroes they can look up to and emulate—real-life heroes and fantasy heroes—heroes who show them what they can grow up to be and imaginary superheroes with amazing powers who fly through the air and right wrongs.

As any family member or teacher knows, much of a young child's learning comes from observing and imitating others. We want children to emulate good behavior and interactions. And that is not always easy to accomplish especially for boys.

Boys need male influences to figure out how men are supposed to act. But, many boys do not have positive male role models. According to the U.S. Census Bureau report *America's Families and Living Arrangements: 2007*, 22 percent of boys under 18 live with a single mother. Many never see their fathers or see them infrequently. Chances are a woman is their teacher in school, too. Many boys look to the media or their neighborhoods for older males to imitate or follow—places where they often find plenty of negative male influences.

That is where heroes and superheroes come in. Boys need men to look up to—real-life heroes who demonstrate such good values as honesty, integrity, compassion, high ideals, hard work, and dependability—and fantasy superheroes who fight for the right, for others, and for justice.

It is especially important that early learning teachers understand this and ensure that young boys have the opportunity to observe good male role models in the classroom—and to act out good values through dramatic superhero play. At this age, young boys begin to form their values and perceptions of the world around them. And that includes their impressions of what makes a man a man.

Feature Real-Life Heroes Boys Can Look Up To

Many boys have fathers, brothers, grandfathers, or uncles who teach them right from wrong, show them how to behave, play ball with them, and demonstrate the value of hard work and education. Unfortunately, many boys are without a stable male presence or live with men who do not pass on admirable qualities. Who do these boys look up to? Chances are their heroes are the sports and entertainment figures they see on television—or older boys and men from the neighborhood who may or may not be good influences.

Exposing boys to male "heroes" who demonstrate good values, are kind and loving, and share and show them what they can grow up to be is essential. Introduce boys to doctors, firefighters, businessmen, policemen, teachers, high school and college students from the community, and men who have made a difference in our country's history or in science, medicine, literature, and art.

All boys benefit when teachers ensure that boys see exemplary males of all ages, races, and occupations in the classroom—whether they are there in person or in books or on posters. This brings a positive male dynamic into classrooms usually run by female teachers, exposes boys to a variety of interesting occupations, and demonstrates the value of education and hard work. Bringing men in to read to the children shows boys that men value reading (It is not just for girls!). Male mentors are particularly influential on boys.

Positive male role models are key to shaping young boys' identities, fostering positive growth, and helping them achieve. They help boys develop high expectations, see opportunities outside their own neighborhood, and recognize realistic opportunities for success beyond sports or entertainment stardom, occupations where only a tiny, tiny percentage of people are successful.

What to Do

- Read stories of real-life heroes of all races and ethnic groups represented in the classroom, including historic and sports persons, people from a variety of occupations, and people who have had to overcome handicaps and other obstacles.
- Ask boys who the heroes are in their everyday lives. What makes someone a hero? Have boys think of people who are everyday heroes. Ask boys if they know anyone they think is a hero. Ask them what makes someone a hero. (Try to steer them away from people who are famous on television and movies and toward those who help or sacrifice for others, try to make their neighborhood or country a better place, or help other people, or friends and family who do nice things for them.)
- Invite males to participate in classroom and special activities. Find ways to involve exemplary men in your program. Hire male aides, recruit male volunteers, and bring in fathers and other men with interesting occupations to talk about what they do.
- Ask male volunteers to read to the children. Having men read books in the classroom shows boys that men value reading.
- Display pictures of heroes. Include pictures of heroes of all races, cultures, genders, occupations, ages, and so on. It bears repeating that special attention should be given to

ensuring that African American and Hispanic/Latino "heroes" are well represented; this is often neglected in today's classrooms and is crucial to the self-identity of boys from these cultures. We have included some ideas in the earlier chapters on African American and Hispanic/Latino boys.

- Promote father-friendly programs. Go out of your way to invite fathers to participate in programs. Make them feel welcome. Develop special activities for fathers and sons.
- Stress the importance of positive role models to families, and provide them with information. If good role models do not exist in boys' homes or neighborhoods, suggest they contact organizations like Big Brothers Big Sisters or look in their community to find mentors or adult males who can spend quality time with the boys

The most important role models in people's lives, it seems, aren't superstars or household names. They're everyday people who quietly set examples for you—coaches, teachers, parents. People about whom you say to yourself, perhaps not even consciously, "I want to be like that."

—TIM FOLEY,
Miami Dolphins

Incorporate Constructive Superhero Play

In homes and early learning classrooms across the United States, little boys are pretending to be Power Rangers or Spider-Man. Boys love their superheroes. It is natural. Throughout history, myths and legends have inspired boys to follow superhuman heroes such as Hercules.

Despite this, teachers often are reluctant to encourage superhero play, assuming boys will tear around their classrooms, thrusting pretend swords at each other and hurting themselves or their classmates. But superhero play can be valuable. Today's superheroes exemplify traits we hope boys will adopt:

- They fight for what is right.
- They protect people.
- They have special powers.
- They use brains before brawn.
- They exercise self-control.
- They care about other people.
- They use their powers for the good of all people.
- They exemplify constructive behavior.

Well-orchestrated superhero play stimulates boys' imaginations and creativity, develops empathy, builds confidence, helps confront fears and anxieties, and builds an understanding of boys' roles in society. With the right guidance, it can even help boys overcome natural tendencies such as impulsiveness, aggression, and lagging verbal skills. For boys from unstable environments, superhero play can help them feel more in control. And it expends some of that seemingly limitless "boy energy."

In incorporating superhero play, you want to make sure the right lessons are learned. So it is important to prepare carefully.

What to Do

- Determine the lessons you want the children to learn from superhero play, and set goals. This will be helpful in determining how you use superhero play in your classroom.
- Establish clear rules and boundaries. Establish rules for superhero play, emphasizing safety and respect for other children. There should be different rules for indoor and outdoor play, based on space requirements. Repeat several times.
- Have a "superhero corner." Identify a safe, indoor place where boys can dress up as superheroes and engage in limited dramatic play (and where all the children can dress up based on their interests). If you have access to a large indoor space—and outdoors—boys can engage in more active superhero play and use their large motor skills.
- Emphasize the prosocial qualities of superheroes, mention well-known

superheroes, and ask the children what superheroes do. Guide the conversation by having them discuss the good they do and how they help other people (showing boys that weapons do not define superheroes). Ask children what they can do to be superheroes and what superhero traits they can use to help their family, teachers, classmates, pets, school, neighborhood, and so on.

- Have a series of lessons on superheroes. What does it mean to be a superhero? Who are the children's superheroes, and why? Help boys understand that a superhero is special because he uses his superpowers to help people in need. Include African American and Hispanic superheroes as noted below.
- Introduce boys to superhero words to build their vocabulary (for example, *hero/villain, strong/helpless, props/scenery, story line/script, peaceful/violent*).
- Have children make up their own superheroes. Have each child take one superhero trait and come up with a superhero that exemplifies that trait (for example, SuperSon, HelperBoy, CatRescuer).
- Read appropriate stories about superheroes. Be sure to include African American superheroes (Captain Brainstorm, Static Shock, Luke Cage, Black Lightning, Falcon, and Patriot) and Hispanic/Latino superheroes (Gangbuster Jose Delgado, El Castigo, El Muerto, Iman, Dora, and Diego) as well as the better-known Superman, Batman, Spider-Man, and so on.
- Let boys create and illustrate their own stories. Ask them to tell you their stories, then write them down and have the boys draw pictures to illustrate them.
- Have capes and gear for boys to act out superhero stories. Include superhero capes, costumes, dolls, puppets, and props. Encourage boys to act out their own superhero stories.
- Work with boys to create a superhero play. Help children create a play where they act out various parts—superhero, villain, people/animals in distress. Create costumes, props, and scenery. You might even want to record the play and show it to families.
- Use superheroes to launch studies of other topics. Start talking about Batman to lead into studies of bats, Spider-Man to study spiders, and Superman to study planets.

- Have a "superhero day" when the boys dress as their favorite superheroes, read stories, and talk about superhero qualities. Have them make up a superhero story or play, and invite families to the performance.
- Give boys opportunities to exercise power and control. Ask boys to make good choices like superheroes do. Give them opportunities to decide where they play and with whom, what to read, when to move from one activity area to another, and who they would like to play in a superhero scenario.
- Stress peaceful solutions to problems. Help boys in conflict arrive at a resolution, as a superhero would.
- Post a superhero chart. List children who have done something special for a classmate, helped a teacher, resolved a conflict, exhibited exemplary behavior, or accomplished a goal.
- Establish a weekly superhero award for a child who most exemplifies a superhero for that week—for anything from creating a superhero story to helping another child.

A DAY TO CELEBRATE SUPERHEROES

Cleveland's Friendly Inn Enrichment Center took the superhero theme to a new level, holding a center-wide Superhero Day aimed at teaching superhero qualities and characteristics—caring, kindness, compassion, helpfulness, protecting others, and protecting themselves.

Everyone participated to make the event successful—the administrator, staff, family members, and children. The children created their own individual superhero masks; the staff collected superhero stories, movies, coloring sheets, and posters. Family members, contacted well in advance, discussed the qualities of superheroes with their children at home. The children were asked what makes someone a superhero and what they can do to be superheroes at home and in their community.

When Superhero Day finally came, the excited children gleefully donned their superhero masks, participated in superhero-themed activities, listened to stories, and responded with their own personal tales of superheroes in their own lives, discussing what made them superheroes.

The teachers are continuing to reinforce the superhero theme with language, activities, and discussions—all aimed at connecting these concepts to the children's daily lives. The posters, too, are staying up on the walls.

RESOURCES USED IN THIS CHAPTER

Bauer, Karen L., and Ernest Dettore. 1997. "Superhero Play: What's a Teacher to Do?" *Early Childhood Education Journal 25*(1): 17–21.

Griffin, Larry. 2010. Notes to author, April 17 (Unpublished).

Kreider, Rose, and Diana Elliott. 2009. *America's Families and Living Arrangements: 2007.* Washington, DC: U.S. Census Bureau. http://www.census.gov/prod/2009pub/p20-561.pdf.

Martin, Justin F. 2007. "Children's Attitudes toward Superheroes as a Potential Indicator of Their Moral Understanding." *Journal of Moral Education* 36(2): 239–250.

IN CONCLUSION

Without a doubt, parents, other family members, teachers, coaches, mental health professionals, and other adults who work with children and youth need to consider brain science in constructing learning environments and crafting activities.

Frequently, however, these measurable learning differences are not taken into consideration. Far too often, females and males are educated as if both process information and experience the same way. Girls, for instance, tend to tolerate and even flourish in environments and with female teachers who use verbal strategies to communicate content—read, read, read, talk, talk, talk, and write, write, write.

Most boys do not thrive in these environments or with teachers who require them to sit in chairs for long periods of time, listen, use words, and keep their minds focused. Clearly, this one-size-fits-all approach is implicated in the trouble that too many of our sons experience in schools. The approach also accounts for a great many of the behavior problems cited by teachers. If troubling trends are to be reversed, we must translate brain-based research into practice to create responsive environments and educational strategies that nurture every child—especially our boys.

Everyone benefits.

ABOUT STARTING POINT

Starting Point is the child care and early education resource and referral agency for four counties in northeastern Ohio: Cuyahoga (Metropolitan Cleveland), Geauga, Lake, and Ashtabula. This agency was one of the first in the United States to address the issues surrounding child care/early education and to develop comprehensive programming to improve quality and increase capacity, access, and affordability. Starting Point has long been an innovator, and many of the agency's programs have been adopted by other organizations, both in Ohio and across the nation.

For northeastern Ohio, Starting Point is an invaluable resource for early childhood professionals, parents, and the community at large, addressing a vast spectrum of early childhood and youth issues, developing and coordinating programs, and offering a wide array of services to

- link families with early childhood centers, family child care homes, and after-school programs;
- increase the number of quality early childhood centers and family child care homes to meet emerging community needs;
- improve the quality of care;
- stimulate early care/education alternatives;
- advocate for children, families, and professionals in the early childhood and youth areas;
- educate consumers, professionals, employers, and the community at large on early childhood and youth issues;
- provide training and technical assistance to child care professionals in supporting and caring for children, including those with medical, developmental, and social/emotional and behavioral needs; and
- collect data on child care/early education needs, services, and gaps.

STARTING POINT FOR CHILD CARE AND EARLY EDUCATION

4600 Euclid Avenue, Suite 500, Cleveland, Ohio 44103 USA
216.575.0061 * 800.880.0971 * www.starting-point.org

ABOUT THE AUTHOR

Ruth Hanford Morhard *has been involved in early childhood education for more than 25 years. She was a consultant to the initial Child Day Care Planning Project, a landmark public-private partnership in Cuyahoga County, Ohio, that addressed the issues of child care and early education and led to the formation of Starting Point, which she has continued to serve in the same capacity. She is president of Ruth Reid & Company; serves as a consultant to national, regional, and local educational and human-service institutions; and is a writer with several books, award-winning publications, films, and videos to her credit. She lives in Chardon, Ohio, has a BA from Skidmore College, and has engaged in graduate study at Stanford University and Case Western Reserve University.*

HANDOUTS FOR PARENTS AND OTHER CAREGIVERS

In this section, you will find tips for parents on raising young boys and limiting media time. We hope you will make copies and distribute them to the parents and other caregivers of the children in your programs.

TIPS FOR PARENTS

Helping Your Boy Be His Best

1. Communicate the importance of education.
2. Help him identify his hopes and dreams for the future.
3. Set realistic and specific goals.
4. Learn about and use boy-friendly strategies at home.
5. Communicate daily with his teacher.
6. Establish daily routines to develop good habits.
7. Make sure he has good male role models.
8. Read to him and let him see you read. Get a library card.
9. Work with his teacher to ensure consistent approaches to learning at home and in school.
10. Offer praise and encouragement.
11. Use television and media wisely.
12. Help create positive peer relationships.
13. Get involved with his early childhood program—attend conferences and activities, or volunteer.
14. Network and connect with parents/ families with similar goals.
15. Get him involved in constructive boy-friendly programs in your community.

Tips for Parents

Boosting Your Boy's Brain

Boys' Brain Tendencies	What Parents Can Do
1. Spatial/mechanical abilities	Provide large play space
	Lots of blocks, construction materials
2. Less verbal ability	Learn by manipulating objects, movement
	Reinforce learning with games, videos
	Read books about heroes, animals, boys
3. Need to move	Space for physical activity inside and out
	Alternate sedentary and physical activities
	Allow some physical bonding
4. Single focus	Let boys stay with activities they like
	Ease them into changes
5. Vision is best sense	Provide good lighting
6. Lack of eye contact	Touch gently to get attention
	Maintain eye contact
7. Difficulty remembering instructions	Repeat directions
	Reinforce using visuals
8. Aggressive behavior	Defuse energy
	Give specific alternative actions
	Read them books on proper behavior
9. Taking risks	Redirect to other activities
	Ensure safe environment
	Give choices
10. Inattention	Give "brain breaks"

Tips for Parents

Making Good Media Choices

1. Limit the amount of screen time for children.
   - None for children zero to two years.
   - One to two hours maximum for children three to five years.
   - No video games for children under seven years.
   - No TVs in children's bedrooms.
2. Have rules on times when TV, videos, and DVDs are allowed, and communicate these clearly to children.
3. Watch media with children, and talk about content.
4. Carefully monitor the programs, music, and films children watch, listen to, or see.
   - Check ratings of TV programs for young children (www.tvguidelines.org/ratings.htm).
   - Restrict violent programs; teach children alternatives to violence.
   - Help children distinguish between fantasy and reality.
   - Turn television off when not watching specific programs.
   - Block unwanted media (TVguidelines.org/parentalcontrols.htm).
5. Ask these questions about any media you are considering for your child:
   - Is this content appropriate?
   - What does this teach my child?
   - What will my child take away from this?
6. Develop a family media usage strategy, including the following:
   - Review your family's current media use.
   - Consider the ages and needs of your children.
   - Educate yourself about children's media.
   - Select age-appropriate, constructive media programming.
   - Teach children media literacy skills.

Adapted from Levin, Douglas, Sousan Arafeh, Carla Baker Deniz, and Julie Gottesman. 2004. *Navigating the Children's Media Landscape: A Parent's and Caregiver's Guide.* Washington DC: Cable in the Classroom.

Resources

I. Recommended Books for Young Boys

The following books are recommended as appropriate for young boys. We have added special sections on books that are especially appropriate for African American and Hispanic/Latino boys and should be integral to all early childhood reading, whatever the racial or ethnic makeup of the group.

A. For All Young Boys

1. Storybooks

Aesop's Fables

Alexander and the Terrible, Horrible, No Good, Very Bad Day by Judith Viorst

Anansi and the Moss-Covered Rock by Eric A. Kimmel

Andy and the Lion by James Daugherty

The Artist Who Painted a Blue Horse by Eric Carle

At Daddy's on Saturdays by Linda Walvoord Girard, with illustrations by Judith Friedman

Ben's Trumpet by Rachel Isadora

The Big Orange Splot by Daniel Manus Pinkwater

The Boy Who Held Back the Sea by Thomas Locker

The Butter Battle Book by Dr. Seuss

The Day Jimmy's Boa Ate the Wash by Trinka H. Noble

Drummer Boy by Ann Warren Turner

The Emperor's New Clothes by Hans Christian Andersen

Goodnight, Goodnight, Construction Site by Sherri Duskey Rinker

Grandfather's Journey by Allen Say

I Can't Wait by Elizabeth Crary, with illustrations by Marina Megale

If You Take a Mouse to School by Laura Numeroff, with illustrations by Felicia Bond

In the Small, Small Pond by Denise Fleming

In the Tall, Tall Grass by Denise Fleming

Island Baby by Holly Keller

Leo the Late Bloomer by Robert Kraus

Lucky Song by Vera B. Williams

The Man Who Kept His Heart in a Bucket by Sonia Levitin

Mean Soup by Betsy Everitt

Mike Mulligan and His Steam Shovel by Virginia L. Burton

Mouse Paint by Ellen Stoll Walsh

The Paper Crane by Molly Garrett Bang

The Polar Express by Chris Van Allsburg

There Was an Old Lady Who Swallowed a Fly by Simms Taback

There's a Nightmare in My Closet by Mercer Mayer

The Three Billy Goats Gruff by P. C. Asbjornsen and J. E. Mos

We're Going on a Bear Hunt by Michael Rosen and Helen
    Oxenbury

What About Me? by Eileen Kennedy-Moore, with illustrations by
    Mits Katayama

2. Humor

Bark, George by Jules Feiffer

Click, Clack, Moo: Cows That Type by Doreen Cronin

Don't Let the Pigeon Drive the Bus! (series) by Mo Willems

Pete's a Pizza by William Steig

3. Nonfiction/Biographies

26 Letters and 99 Cents by Tana Hoban

Freight Train by Donald Crews

The Story of Abraham Lincoln by Patricia A. Pingry, with
    illustrations by Stephanie McFetridge-Britt

The Story of Benjamin Franklin by Patricia A. Pingry, with
    illustrations by Stephanie McFetridge-Britt

The Story of George Washington by Patricia A. Pingry, with
    illustrations by Stephanie McFetridge-Britt

The Story of Martin Luther King Jr. by Johnny Ray Moore, with
    illustrations by Amy Wummer

The Story of Thomas Jefferson by Patricia A. Pingry, with
    illustrations by Meredith Johnson .

Trashy Town by Andrea Zimmerman and David Clemesha

The Z Was Zapped by Chris Van Allsburg

4. Dinosaurs

Baby Triceratops by Beth Spanjian

Bones, Bones, Dinosaur Bones by Byron Barton

Curious George and the Dinosaur by H. A. Rey

The Day of the Dinosaur by Stan and Jan Berenstain, with
    illustrations by Michael Berenstain

Dinosaur Babies by Maida Silverman

Dinosaur Day by Liza Donnelly

The Dinosaur Who Lived in My Backyard by B. G. Hennessy

Dinosaurs (a First Discovery Science book from Scholastic)

Dinosaurs by Gail Gibbons

Dinosaurs, Dinosaurs by Byron Barton

My Visit to the Dinosaurs by Aliki

Patrick's Dinosaurs by Carol Carrick

Whatever Happened to the Dinosaurs? by Bernard Most

5. Animals and Nature

All About Seeds by Susan Kuchalla

Animals and Their Babies (from Macmillan Early Science books)

Bugs! Bugs! Bugs! by Bob Barner

The Carrot Seed by Ruth Krauss

The Caterpillar and the Polliwog by Jack Kent

Chickens Aren't the Only Ones by Ruth Heller

The Egg (a First Discovery Science book from Scholastic)

Flowers (a First Discovery Science book from Scholastic)

A Friend for Einstein, the Smallest Stallion by Charlie Cantrell

Giraffes Can't Dance by Giles Andreae

The Grouchy Ladybug by Eric Carle

Growing Vegetable Soup by Lois Ehlert

How Ducklings Grow by Diane Molleson

How Rocket Learned to Read by Tad Hills

Lyle, Lyle Crocodile by Bernard Waber

Martha Speaks by Susan Meddaugh

Owl Babies by Martin Waddell

Planting a Rainbow by Lois Ehlert

The Reason for a Flower by Ruth Heller

Red Leaf, Yellow Leaf by Lois Ehlert

See How It Grows by Marguerite Walters

Seeds Get Around (from Macmillan Early Science books)

Shark vs. Train by Chris Barton

A Sick Day for Amos McGee by Philip C. Stead

Skeletons! Skeletons! All about Bones by Katy Hall

The Snail and the Whale by Julia Donaldson

Stars by Mary Lyn Ray

Stellaluna by Janell Cannon

The Story of Ferdinand by Munro Leaf

The Tiny Seed by Eric Carle

Tree (a First Discovery Science book from Scholastic)

What Do You Do with a Tail Like This? by Steve Jenkins and
    Robin Page

6. Sports

Little Granny Quarterback by Bill Martin Jr., Michael Sampson,
    and Michael Chesworth

Swish! by Bill Martin Jr., Michael Sampson, and Michael
    Chesworth

7.   Mystery and Adventure

How I Became a Pirate by Melinda Long

I Spy (series) by Jean Marzollo and Walter Wick

Oh, the Places You'll Go! by Dr. Seuss

Smash! Crash! Trucktown (series) by Jon Scieszka, David
    Shannon, Loren Long, and David Gordon

8. Fantasy, Superheroes

The Adventures of Sparrowboy by Brian Pinkney

Harold and the Purple Crayon by Crockett Johnson

I'm Going to Be the Best Superhero Ever! by Moira Butterfield,
    with illustrations by Caroline Davis

A Little Hero in the Making by Emilie Barnes, with illustrations
    by Michael Sparks

SuperHero ABC by Bob McLeod

When a Dragon Moves In by Jodi Moore

Where the Wild Things Are by Maurice Sendak

9. Poetry and Wordplay

Chicka Chicka Boom Boom by Bill Martin Jr. and John
    Archambault

Is Your Mama a Llama? by Deborah Guarino

Jamberry by Bruce Degen

Llama Llama Red Pajama by Anna Dewdney

Pierre: A Cautionary Tale by Maurice Sendak

10. Feelings and Relationships

A Book of Love for Mothers and Sons by Rob D. Walker

Daddy's Lullaby by Tony Bradman

The Good-Bye Book by Judith Viorst

Guess How Much I Love You by Sam McBratney

How to Lose All Your Friends by Nancy Carlson

I Want It by Elizabeth Crary

I'm Excited by Elizabeth Crary

I'm Frustrated by Elizabeth Crary

I'm Furious by Elizabeth Crary

I'm Mad by Elizabeth Crary

I'm Proud by Elizabeth Crary

I'm Scared by Elizabeth Crary

Mommy, Don't Go by Elizabeth Crary, with illustrations by Marina Megale

No, David! (series) by David Shannon

The Tenth Good Thing about Barney by Judith Viorst

Tickle Monster Laughter Kit by Josie Bissett

When You're Silly and You Know It by Elizabeth Crary and Shari Steelsmith, with illustrations by Mits Katayama

B. Especially for Young African-American Boys

All Aboard! by Mary Lyn Ray

Allie's Basketball Dream by Barbara E. Barber, with illustrations by Darryl Ligasan

Black All Around! by Patricia Hubbell

Bring on That Beat by Rachel Isadora

A Chair for My Mother by Vera B. Williams

Clean Your Room, Harvey Moon! by Pat Cummings

Daddy Calls Me Man by Angela Johnson

Do You Know What I'll Do? by Charlotte Zolotow

Full, Full, Full of Love by Trish Cooke

Grandfather and I by Helen Elizabeth Buckley

He's Got the Whole World in His Hands by Kadir Nelson

Hewitt Anderson's Great Big Life by Jerdine Nolen

Hip Hop Dog by Chris Raschka

Hot Day on Abbott Avenue by Karen English

Kente Colors by Debbi Chocolate

Kevin and His Dad by Irene Smalls

Max's Starry Night by Ken Wilson-Max

Mufaro's Beautiful Daughters: An African Tale retold by John Steptoe

My Family Plays Music by Judy Cox

My Freight Train by Michael Rex

The Neighborhood Mother Goose by Nina Crews

One Hot Summer Day by Nina Crews

Peekaboo Morning by Rachel Isadora

Please, Baby, Please by Tonya Lewis Lee

Please, Puppy, Please by Tonya Lewis Lee

Rap a Tap Tap by Leo Dillon

Shades of Black by Sandra L. Pinkney

The Snowy Day by Ezra Jack Keats

Sunday Best by Juwanda G. Ford, with illustrations by Colin Boo

This Jazz Man by Karen Ehrhardt

The Two Tyrones by Wade Hudson, with illustrations by Mark Page

Uh-oh! by Rachel Isadora

What's What? A Guessing Game by Mary Serfozo

When Will Sarah Come? by Elizabeth Fitzgerald Howard

Whistle for Willie by Ezra Jack Keats

Whoever You Are by Mem Fox, with illustrations by Leslie Staub

Why Mosquitoes Buzz in People's Ears: A West African Tale by Verna Aardema

Yo, Jo! by Rachel Isadora

Zomo the Rabbit: A Trickster Tale from West Africa by Gerald McDermott

C. **Especially for Young Hispanic/Latino Boys**

Abuela by Arthur Dorros

Arrorró, Mi Niño: Latino Lullabies and Gentle Games by Lulu Delacre

Arroz con Leche: Popular Songs and Rhymes from Latin America by Lulu Delacre

Book Fiesta! by Pat Mora

Borreguita and the Coyote by Verna Aardema

The Bossy Galileo: A Traditional Cuban Folk Tale by Lucia M. Gonzalez

Chato's Kitchen (La cocina del Chato) by Gary Soto

Cuckoo-Cucú: A Folktale from Mexico/Cuckoo-Cucú: Un cuento folklórico mexicano by Lois Ehlert

Gathering the Sun: An Alphabet in Spanish and English by Alma Flor Ada

Just in Case: A Trickster Tale and Spanish Alphabet Book by Yuyi Morales

My Mexico by Tony Johnston

Nacho and Lolita by Pam Munoz Ryan

Perez and Martina by Pura Belpre

Quinito, Day and Night/Quinito, dia y noche by Ina Cumpiano

What Can You Do with a Paleta? by Carmen Tafolla

Yagua Days by Cruz Martel

II. RECOMMENDED BOOKS FOR EARLY CHILDHOOD PROFESSIONALS AND INTERESTED PARENTS/FAMILIES

African American Males in School and Society by Vernon C. Polite and James Earl Davis

Awakening the Natural Genius of Black Children by Amos Wilson

Beyond Centers and Circle Time by Pamela Phelps

Black Children: Coping in a Racist Society by Alvin Poussaint

Black Children: Their Roots, Culture, and Learning Styles by Janice E. Hale-Benson

A Black Parent's Handbook to Educating Your Children (Outside of the Classroom) by Baruti K. Kafele

Boys and Girls Learn Differently! A Guide for Teachers and Parents by Michael Gurian

Brain Sex: The Real Difference between Men and Women by Anne Moir and David Jessel

Countering the Conspiracy to Destroy Black Boys by Jawanza Kunjufu

Enriching the Brain by Eric Jensen

Grand Theft Childhood: The Surprising Truth about Violent Video Games and What Parents Can Do by Lawrence Kutner and Cheryl K. Olson

Helping Boys Succeed in School by Terry W. Neu and Rich Weinfeld

Hip-Hop vs. MAAT: A Psycho/Social Analysis of Values by Jawanza Kunjufu

Hispanic Foodways, Nutrition, and Health by Diva Sanjur

The Hispanic Way: Aspects of Behavior, Attitudes, and Customs of the Spanish-Speaking World by J. Noble and J. LaCasa

How to Teach Math to Black Students by Shahid Muhammad

Into the Minds of Babes: How Screen Time Affects Children from Birth to Age Five by Lisa Guernsey

It's Not Only Rock & Roll by Donald Roberts and Peter Christenson

Keeping Black Boys Out of Special Education by Jawanza Kunjufu

Kill Them Before They Grow: Misdiagnosis of African American Boys in American Classrooms by Michael Porter

Leadership and the Sexes by Barbara Annis and Michael Gurian

Learning While Black: Creating Educational Excellence for African American Children by Janice E. Hale

Losing the Race: Self-Sabotage in Black America by John H. McWhorter

Magnificent Mind at Any Age by Daniel Amen

The Male Brain by Louann Brizendine

The Men They Will Become by Eli H. Newberger

The Minds of Boys: Saving Our Sons from Falling Behind in School and Life by Michael Gurian

Navigating the Children's Media Landscape: A Parent's and Caregiver's Guide by American Institutes for Research. Available online at www.air.org/files/CableChildMediaGuide.pdf.

Nurture the Nature by Michael Gurian

Peace in the Streets, Breaking the Cycle of Gang Violence by Arturo Hernandez

The Purpose of Boys: Helping Our Sons Find Meaning, Significance, and Direction in Their Lives by Michael Gurian

Raising Black Children by James P. Comer and Alvin F. Poussaint

Raising Respectful Children in a Disrespectful World by Jill Rigby

Sex on the Brain by Daniel Amen

Single Mamahood: Advice and Wisdom for the African American Single Mother by Kelly Williams

Sociology by Richard T. Schaefer

Teaching Hispanic Children by Toni Grigo Jones and Mary Lou Fuller

Through Ebony Eyes: What Teachers Need to Know but Are Afraid to Ask About African American Students by Gail L. Thompson

Why Boys Fail: Saving Our Sons from an Educational System That's Leaving Them Behind by Richard Whitmire

III. RECOMMENDED WEBSITES FOR EARLY CHILDHOOD PROFESSIONALS

Coalition of Schools Educating Boys of Color

www.coseboc.org

A coalition of schools dedicated to equipping boys of color to achieve academically, socially, and emotionally through research and promising practices modeled in participating schools.

Gurian Institute

www.gurianinstitute.com

A leader in educating and training teachers and parents in the ways boys and girls learn differently and in offering strategies to enhance the potential of each gender. Numerous books available.

HARVARD UNIVERSITY CENTER ON THE DEVELOPING CHILD

www.developingchild.harvard.edu

Conducts research and designs, implements, and evaluates innovative program and practice models to improve life outcomes for children.

KAPLAN EARLY LEARNING COMPANY

www.kaplanco.com

Kaplan has long been a leader in early care and education, developing and publishing curriculum and assessment products as well as those that promote learning and play.

NATIONAL ASSOCIATION FOR THE EDUCATION OF YOUNG CHILDREN

www.naeyc.org

The world's largest organization working with and on behalf of children from birth through age eight. NAEYC convenes thought leaders, teachers and other practitioners, researchers, and other stakeholders and sets standards of excellence for programs and teachers in early childhood education.

NATIONAL PUBLIC RADIO: EDUCATING LATINOS

www.npr.org/programs/atc/features/2002/nov/educating_latinos/
series.html

A five-part series on the growing Hispanic population in the United
States, language barrier issues, and educating and assimilating
Latinos and Latinas.

PARENTS' CHOICE

www.parentschoice.org

Offers recommendations and reviews of software, video games,
and interactive toys.

PAS: PROMOTING ACADEMIC SUCCESS OF BOYS OF COLOR

http://pas.fpg.unc.edu

A W. K. Kellogg Foundation project at the University of North
Carolina for implementing and evaluating ways to improve the
academic achievement of boys ages three to eight.

PBS TEACHERS EARLY CHILDHOOD

www.pbs.org/teachers/earlychildhood

Contains articles, activities, thematic units, and learning ideas and
tips for parents and families.

PBS UNDERSTANDING AND RAISING BOYS

www.pbs.org/parents/raisingboys

A guide to helping boys feel more confident, succeed in school,
and grow up resilient and responsible. An outgrowth of the
acclaimed PBS documentary Raising Cain, which explores
issues facing today's boys.

RAISING HIM ALONE

www.raisinghimalone.com

Offering resources and support for mothers raising boys alone.

STARTING POINT

www.starting-point.org

Starting Point offers resources for child care professionals,
parents, and the community at large and develops special
programs and strategies for teaching boys in early learning
classrooms.

IV. CHILD/PARENT SUPPORT/MENTORING ORGANIZATIONS

These organizations can be especially helpful for referrals to single mothers and parents of minority children in your classrooms.

BIG BROTHERS BIG SISTERS
www.bbbs.org/site/c.9iILI3NGKhK6F/b.5961093/k.EC87/Find_a_
    Local_Agency.htm
Matches fatherless children with a responsible adult of the same
    gender to spend time together, attend events, and enjoy one
    another's company. Log on to this link for a local office.

CONCERNED BLACK MEN
www.cbmnational.org/chapters
Provides mentors and programs, offering positive black role
    models for children and their parents. Log on to this link for
    a local affiliate.

NATIONAL LATINO FATHERHOOD & FAMILY INSTITUTE
www.nlffi.org
Provides information and training to help Hispanic/Latino
    fathers develop strong, active roles in the lives of their
    children, families, and community.

NATIONAL ORGANIZATION OF SINGLE MOTHERS (NOSM)
www.singlemothers.org
This networking system helps single mothers meet the
    challenges of daily life with wisdom, dignity, confidence, and
    courage. Annual dues apply.

PROJECT SINGLE MOMS
www.projectsinglemoms.com
Empowerment and education for single moms. A growing
    nonprofit organization with chapters in several cities.

SINGLE PARENT RESOURCE CENTER
http://singleparentusa.com
This site contains a network of single-parent self-help groups,
    along with information and referrals, seminars, consultation,
    and a resource library.

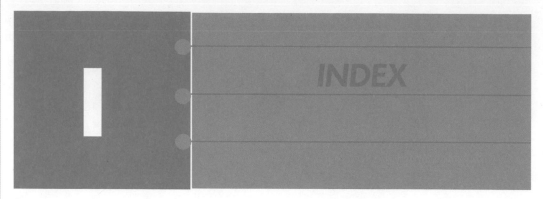

INDEX